# SPIRITUAL ECONOMY

For those in Business with a Moral Conscience

By

Oscar Calderon

# Acknowledgement

I would like to acknowledge Michael Dell, CEO of Dell, Inc. who started his company in Austin, TX and built a model company for business. I served his company for eight years as an employee. At the time, I seized on opportunities available to improve and grow in my technical career, becoming a Dell Systems Engineer and also becoming certified as a Project Management Professional.

I would also like to acknowledge The University of Texas Exes Alumni Association for noticing my abilities in high school and supported my choice to attend The University of Texas at Austin with a kind-hearted Scholarship. I kept my promise to the Association and later graduated with a Bachelor of Science Degree in 1985. This is one the most significant achievements for me because at that moment, I became a third-generation graduate of The University of Texas.

DISCIPLINA
PRAESIDIUM
CIVITATIS

And for those things unseen that strengthen my faith in God

# Dedication

This book is dedicated to my father and his business acumen acquired as an independent pharmacy owner in a small, southwest Texas town. It was my choice to set out and learn all he knew about business and try to carry on what he had started. Facing adversity in 1980, he was forced out of the market by big box, retail pharmacies and had to close his business like a lot of other independent pharmacies. Today, big chain retail pharmacies practice the same methods my father practiced in order to survive, and the market has developed into what is now known as Big Pharma.

He was my mentor and my best friend.

# Table of Contents

# Chapter 1:  Faith and Finance

I am writing this book in an attempt to explain how one may understand and interpret religion and your own existence as you embark to seek further knowledge of what may be considered spiritual.  Since you are placed on this earth and exist in human form, you are taught to live each day by being nurtured and developed into the nature of our environment.  Like in the wilderness, there are methods of survival and that same method exists in this world.  My experience has been that the method of survival involves getting down to the business of living or retiring from a life looked upon from a distant past.  As we develop from being a child, nurtured by family, we see how businesses operate all around us and thrive on the exchange of currency.  Businesses must survive on its production.

Managing this exchange, a business increases revenue, ultimately measuring its value, its methods of existence and therefore, survival.  My parents emphasized that religion would become an important part of my life.  At a certain point in your own life, you will wonder why you are taught different things pertaining to conformity, morality and eventually survival.  They felt that including religion would relatively increase the measurement in value taken of my existence and provide sustenance and longevity through periods of judgement.  A friend once told me we only know what we are taught.

So, it's your decision to seek further knowledge about your own religion and ask how your own thoughts are being developed, practicing your own faith and beliefs.

My own experience has usually involved a church and growing up I noticed that the church was attended with frequency and each time an offering was made in the form of payment or gift of a certain amount of money --- an exchange of currency. I find out that this exchange is a symbol of something you possess in value in exchange for multiple blessings of goodness and safety.

The concept is that the measure of your gift in value will provide an increase in the form of blessings not yet seen or experienced or an exponential increase of the same currency provided as a gift. Yes, this currency can be defined as something other than money and you begin to wonder how long will the value of this currency hold. In the financial world, you can say this is related to an investment --- a contribution with a value, in the form of currency, time, service or labor.

Over time, the expectation is to benefit from a return in the form of dividends or increased value. Say your belief is based on the existence of a deity, and you ask, "How does this relate to a monetary offering I'm giving or a donation I'm making?"

It is the belief that the unseen return will occur as part of your existence. In your own current environment, your presence, allows an understanding that makes an exchange quite tangible.

It's like a real person in relation to you, or somebody related to you. Well, there is such an instrument as inheritance where someone related to you passes down his/her possessions to you for keeps or you become the beneficiary of a life insurance policy. The policy or trust is usually for the loved ones in your life and secures that a portion of your gratitude remains with them, so that you can experience blessings in life yet to be realized. This is what a person will experience when deciding to involve a deity in their life. It's a way to make the belief in a deity more tangible and the hope that a higher power will bring blessings and joy.

Earlier in time when there was no currency, the exchange of trade was made with perishable goods, commodities and livestock. Life insurance then becomes a matter of discussion.

The basis of insurance is to reduce or avoid risk. I have been told that financial investments come with a risk. For instance, purchasing a policy in return for currency in the event you experience loss of property or loss of life. The amount is redeemed at the time the event takes place or at the time of death not yet realized. For property loss, once appraised, the amount given for your loss is the total cost limited by the amount the policy covers, the higher the covered limit makes the policy much more expensive. For life insurance, this is a return you will never see unless what you have been taught on morality does not apply.

A lot of people say that when you die, you can't take your money and belongings with you.

Billy Graham made this a key message asking, "What do you intend to do? Hook up a U-Haul to the back of your hearse at your funeral procession?" When I was introduced into the Christian-Protestant denomination of faith, I was not guilty.

In 1996, I was frustrated with the lack of resources I had available to grow a business. I was [exhausted] and withdrawn 25 years ago. I had some possessions, my dignity and aspiring hope and vigor.

All in the course to learn more about Christian doctrine, I approached a Christian-Protestant/Pentecostal based church and learned that I wasn't going to be allowed to pursue a business much less allowed finances for growth. At the time, I felt involuntarily stripped of all of it and to this day have never recovered. Even at the time I was told over and over that my time has come and I would be blessed with abundance.

Today, I'm brokenhearted, tired, old, weak and uninspired after experiencing personal loss in addition to the pandemic raging the country now. The most important thing I have accomplished in my life is graduating from college, which didn't come easy for me. There has been this lingering force that exists around me since childhood, which attempts to block my efforts to achieve success which started in high school.

I was doing well academically, ranked top ten of my class yet the highest scholarship I was able to receive was $300. When I applied to resources offering scholarships and financial aid, I felt they requested unnecessary tax documents from my father which he couldn't provide.

My father owned an independent pharmacy from 1959-1980 and was able to maintain a modest income at the time and became involved in local politics which he loved. He became a significant member of society and he may have made some enemies along the way. Being the youngest in the family, I had to figure how to pay for my college education when I got accepted into a major university. I was eligible for financial aid, mostly loans and once I received a loan, I was required to take over 15 hours of classes per semester. I chose engineering because I love science. The course-load and class sizes were so large I found it impossible to cram all of the study assignments on my calendar and then retain the content in STEM. I had to decide to remain in Engineering or switch career paths. It didn't matter any which way I turned I would encounter that same force in my way, like a roadblock. I saw my father becoming frail and tired every year trying to support all four of his children attending a major university.

He insisted that I focus on my studies instead of trying to find full time work, something he also experienced at the same university. Yet, I was struggling financially and my brother and I wondered where our next meal would come from. There was a point where I felt I wouldn't be able to manage the next hurdle. The school gave me an ultimatum after two semesters, which was to pass and continue, or fail and be expelled. I remember the exact moment I grew up into adulthood and had to make decisions on my own.

I sought direction from my father whose experience and education had come from the same university when he graduated from the University of Texas School of Pharmacy in 1957. When I told him about my dilemma, he laughed at me together with his pharmacist/colleague. I was hurt in one way, but I understood the reaction. They had gone through the same experience and probably worse treatment at one of the best Pharmacy Schools in the country.

So, I switched to The School of Communications at the same University and found the film school required $1500 to remain in their program. I stayed enrolled in the program even though I didn't have the money for any film production and still managed to finish with a degree --- the prize of which I remained focused on from the beginning. I was also able to minor in Astrophysics with my Science background and with the minimal Spanish language skills I brought with me to college, I also minored in Spanish.

I realize there are tests we are given and those people that offered their meaningful input often told me, "If you fall, just get up brush yourself off and move forward."

Do you ever wonder if God has feelings? I think He does.

The Apostle Paul was inspired to preach the Gospel of John and which says, "For God so ever loved the world that he gave his only son..." I think he was referring to the extent of extreme measures God took to save humanity. Maybe an explanation can be found in the meaning of what Jesus said about loving one another.

You will never understand why he said this unless you have loved someone so much and they don't have the same love for you in return, yet it happens all of the time in marriage. When the flame of love burns out, the relationship ceases to exist and hatred is the result. That breaking point is critical enough to cause a hardening in your heart which eventually affects decisions made on the fate of mankind, declaration of wars and crimes against humanity.

Although I never married, my own experience resulted in ending that relationship after asking for her hand in marriage, and the decision to never see or speak to that person again. That was over 15 years ago and to this day, and I still suffer pain.

People tell me that God has been with me, present, guiding me through trials and tribulations. I'm trying to believe that, instead, I like to think that he distanced himself from me and not just abandoned me, thrown away like a piece of garbage after being molested early on at age 7 by a family relative.

As a young child, I felt devalued and I try to understand why he was absent when I needed protection at such an early age.

When we develop as children, we may not be aware of how much our surrounding and upbringing affects our conscience, but it does affect the outlook of our future. This becomes much more prominent when we begin to compare what we have to other kids, classmates, team-mates, as we attempt to build friendships, interact and play games, or receive the quality of education to prepare us for success.

It's inevitable that you will encounter those that materially have better things than you, or even allow you to interact with certain types of kids.

Some will receive a better education and become better prepared and you begin to realize that you will have to work twice as hard to complete your goals, while others will not have that need. This is when another type of learning takes place, that of survival and determination, when everything else that makes life easier is taken away.

You begin to realize what becomes necessary and what can be considered materialistic. At the same time, maybe you want to follow a path of moral value as opposed to following the crowd down the wrong path.

Today, I've seen so much hypocrisy and corruption from supposed leaders of society that I am convinced that people inherently without question, want and desire to achieve success without regard for doing good. I had to ask church members, "Do people inherently want to do good?" I was told, "Yes." Although I heard a tele-evangelist say that mankind has a nature inclined to engage in bad conduct.

He said that kids today cannot wait to commit sin the minute after they are born. I would gather he said this because we are born into a fallen world. A world that adores the material things that make our life easier.

## Christian Doctrine

I have heard a preacher say we were bought with a price. That a person paid for all our sins and his name is Jesus Christ. This is a reference called the gospel of Jesus Christ brought forth by Apostle Paul. Paul evangelized throughout the world mainly preaching the resurrection of Jesus and life eternal. The Apostle Peter on the other hand, preached the death of Jesus Christ. The thought of being bought and owned brings to mind slavery, those bought and sold for labor. In the sense that one human being is put up for sale, like property, to be used for labor. In this case being "bought with a price" means that we, humans, were purchased as a whole (body and soul) to be preserved for eternity. It is said this is achieved through the blood of Jesus Christ. This can only be true if one has faith, that there is a life beyond death and a higher power is capable of preserving humanity. Otherwise, the belief would be we were sold for another purpose and remain on this earth under the authority of the one who made the purchase.

Slavery has existed throughout history –Jews endured 40 years of slavery under Egyptian rule until Moses came to free them. The Roman Empire known as imperium Romanum, an immense power formed to promote life and all its secret seditions, practiced slavery. The United States practiced slavery and it required a civil war to end the practice. It may have appeared that all the power and lavish lifestyles of the Roman Empire was indeed self-destructive.

Renown philosopher Frederich Nietzsche and his own philosophy describes that power itself is the feeling that enables power over others. Nietzsche went on to describe "happiness" is that feeling, it allows you to overcome resistance. This same "happiness" is what the Romans believed would be robbed if the belief system of immortal life were to be adopted. The world that the Roman Empire created and fought to preserve eventually crumbled under its own self-destructive foundation of corruption, greed, lawlessness and violence.

The Apostle Paul became part of this society and persecuted Christians to uphold what Nietzsche himself described as good. On his way to Damascus, I believe is when Paul realized this. He had converted his evangelical movement using a more nihilistic approach and included apocryphal affects into a religion whose final judgement offers resurrection and eternal life. By using the promise of life after death, Paul was able to turn Christianity from a peace movement of achieving "happiness", into a religion that offers possible resurrection and eternal life. He gained power over the masses by convincing people that there is no meaning to present life, there is only life in the beyond. Present life requires your instincts to grow and survive yet his view of personal immortality destroys natural instinct.

This was a movement that appealed to personal vanity, and so attracted the fallen, those that had failed in life, criminals, prisoners, and masses of lower- class people struggling to make a living.

He evangelized the offering of life after death for everyone and appealed to one's individual ego. The result was a society where there was no interest in the salvation of everyone, only the mere preparation for crucifixion.

This is the inner battle that takes place within a man's soul. When you set out to carry out a meaningful movement and encounter tyrannical rule like the Roman Empire. Paul needed to accept that his very own leader was murdered and continue to carry out the journey he had set forth. Paul and the insurrectionist movement in the name of Jesus of Nazareth against the Jewish church, temples, and the Jewish nation as a whole was seen as a threat to its existence. Considered anarchy, he woke the outcasts and "sinners" and staged a revolt against the established order of things.

This is why it is called the fear of God. The fear that God will never have to bestow his mercy upon you, that you become expendable. We have to look upon these desperate measures of inherent fear to avoid death or judgment.

His mercy can never be denied but only by those living among you. It is said that it can be denied without having his Spirit in you. It is further said that the Spirit is received through the ritual of baptism. An unseen Spirit or Ghost must enter your living being as you live.

Those baptized early in life do so to receive what is supposed to come from a higher power and be defined as set apart or Holy. Early in life we have not yet experienced our surroundings, innocent to those who nurture us. To receive a Spirit early in life allows us to grow with part of something greater, to guide us through development and to conform to an acceptable way of life.

An apparition or ghost may appear later in life and may cause conflict if allowed to enter your existence, so it becomes a learned process to overcome this situation with discernment.

Nevertheless, this is considered a trespass since the ritual of baptism has taken place and there exists a Spirit in you already.

To be overshadowed by an apparition or ghost is by invitation only and an invitation comes by way of sin since it is said that by sin we move further away from God.

**Belief in Immortality**

Does Christianity appeal to your ego? You have to start with the concept of life after death and the premise that there is no meaning to present life.

Living in the beyond means breaking the laws of nature, becoming immortal and obtaining salvation for everyone.

Some would argue that not everyone should deserve salvation asking, "Why are we saving this guy?". It seems to hint toward hypocrisy, elitism and personal vanity. I feel the focus should be to reconstruct the general view of death from an end, rather to a "passing".

This way you can use the elements of science, the concepts of quantum physics and biology to explain away all reason.

**Conforming to a way of living**

As mentioned earlier, when there was no currency, the exchange of trade was made with perishable goods, commodities and livestock. This was the currency used to offer in return for diverting from a way of living that conforms to the lives in this time period. Life in this time period was based on conforming to a way of life of moral or immoral acts. The actions of people were determined whether they were moral enough as to not be considered immoral, or a sin.

The only problem was that this determination is made by a person living among you passing judgment, and you begin to wonder who is making this final decision.

In Romans 2 it says,

*"When you judge others and then do the same things which they do, you condemn yourself."* Do you think you will escape judgement? The belief in a higher power gives us hope that this judgement is neutral and fair.

Since societies before Christianity involved paganism and the belief in multiple deities, a range of immoral behavior existed depending upon which God among many was being worshipped. Greek mythology and its understanding provided depictions and scenarios of how a common mortal man can relate to the complexities of living in a civilized world.

I would say it is the more accurate account in early civilization of explaining the dynamic of mortality and immortality, the divine and the physical world. Being polytheistic meant that different meaning and understanding were applied to different civilizations creating a range of beliefs and ideology.

The Roman Empire most likely adopted this ideology although encountered major conflict and lack of consensus among the masses. Since the Roman Catholic Church was developed at the time of Jesus's death, the adoption of beliefs in one God was accepted. It is said that the Catholic Church was formed by the Apostle Peter, with the collection of the blood of the Jesus.

This is confirmed in Sunday mass and confirmation of this belief is made every Sunday during the recital of The Profession of Faith as follows:

# The Profession of Faith

*I believe in one God, the Father almighty, maker of heaven and earth, of all the things seen and unseen. I believe in the Lord Jesus Christ, the Only Begotten Son of God, born of the Father before all ages. God from God, Light from Light, true God from true God, begotten, not made, one in being with the Father; through him all things were made. For us men and for our salvation he came down from heaven, and by the Holy Spirit was born of the Virgin Mary and became a man. For our sake he was crucified and died under Pontius Pilate, he suffered, died and was buried, and rose again on the third day in fulfillment of the Scriptures. He ascended into heaven and is seated at the right hand of the Father. He will come again in glory to judge the living and the dead and his kingdom will have no end. I believe in the Holy Spirit, the Lord, the giver of life, who proceeds from the Father and the Son, with the Father and the Son he is worshipped and glorified. He has spoken through the prophets. I believe in one, holy, catholic and apostolic Church. I acknowledge one Baptism for the forgiveness of sins, and I look for the resurrection of the dead and the life of the world to come.*
*Amen.*

The definition of sin, from my learning is to fall short of the expectations set by a higher power. Having the hope of attaining these expectations brought a new self-confidence to those living in fear, for fear of punishment from the Gods.

Meanwhile in the Americas, pagan rituals continued with human sacrifice taking place among civilizations as a way of pleasing the Gods. The Mayans, Incas, and Olmecs all practiced pagan rituals around 300 BC and carried well into the Aztec civilizations which were known to worship the sun God. In the Middle East, Re, also God of the Sun was to have reigned in Egypt, uncharacteristically adopting a monotheistic society.

The Old Testament brought forth the Ten Commandments considered "The Law." It was found that man is unable to follow and adhere to the "shall and shall not" items included on the list.

It is imperative to mention that the First Commandment as recorded in **Exodus 20:3** states, *"Thou shall have no other gods before me. Thou shalt not make unto thee any graven image, or any likeness of anything that is in heaven or that is in the water or under the earth. Thou shall not bow down thyself to them, nor serve them: For I am the LORD your God and I tolerate no rivals. I bring punishment on those who hate me and, on their descendants down to the third and fourth generation. But I show my love to thousands of generations of those who love me and obey my laws."*

From **Romans 3:9**, *"There is no one who is righteous, no one who is wise or who worships God. All have turned away from God; they have all gone wrong; no one does what is right, not even one."*

This gives control to the originator of His commandments although, **verse 20** states: *"For no one is put right in God's sight by doing what the Law requires; what the Law does is to make us know that we have sinned."*

Simply, being made aware that our actions are not in alignment with what God wants for us. This refers to your own self-conscience.

Having the sense of conscience to follow these commandments in your thought process that eventually leads you to act and behave in a civilized society.

## Chapter 2: Moral Compass in Business

Morality (from Latin moralitas 'manner, character, proper behavior'). Intentions, decisions and actions that are considered right or wrong. Webster's dictionary defines it as "conformity to ideals of right human conduct." When one conforms to conduct there is usually a set of standards or principles being followed from a particular philosophy, religion or culture. Furthermore, there may exist a doctrine or system of moral conduct which is more related to principles of right and wrong in behavior.

Aristotle recognized tragedy as the catalyst to cleanse the soul, as opposed to Schopenhauer's philosophy placing pity as the highest virtue of all. Aristotle was a key figure in laying the foundation for modern science. His father was Nicomachus and died when he was child. Aristotle was brought up by a guardian and became a mentor to Alexander the Great. He later joined Plato's Academy until the age of 37. At the beginning of 343 BC, he established a library in Lyceum and helped to produce a number of books on scrolls. This devotion to a library shows leaders like Aristotle lived a disciplined life of learning and should be emulated.

At the core of Christianity is the bearing of the cross. Carrying your burden of transgression and sin and leaving the cross on the mount. It is most likely an act to atone for sins and plead for God's mercy.

This probably best describes the development of Schopenhauer's philosophy from his subconscious point of view found in **Luke 14:11**, *"For everyone who exalts himself will be humbled, and he who humbles himself will be exalted."*

In **Peter 5:5**, about pride and humility, *"When pride comes, then comes disgrace, but with the humble is wisdom"* and in **Peter 5:6**, *"Humble yourselves, therefore, under the mighty hand of God so that at the proper time he may exalt you."*

The cross represents the shame involved in carrying that burden. I met someone who showed me her sketch art. I was amazed, beautiful renditions in sketch form, and I asked her to sketch a piece of art for me. She smiled and obliged. I told her to sketch two crosses on a hill or mount, one without the body of Jesus and one with the body of Jesus. I said, "As an artist, I would like for you to show which cross is more important to you". She finished the sketch, a beautiful work of art, and she displayed prominence on the cross with the body of Jesus on it. This is what the artist projected on the canvass. I accepted the sketch with gratitude and was in awe of its beauty. As I studied the sketch, I kept my eye on the lone cross in the background, aesthetically deeper in focus and smaller, and my preference or rendering was to have the cross itself displayed as the prominent subject. I am divulging my true understanding of the Christian religion when I feel that the lone cross has a more prominent meaning for me.

There is no body. My burden does not require a living, breathing body on the cross. Why would some argue that it does?

Those that adhere to the Gospel, support that it does. The Apostle Paul created a construct of recognizing the death of Jesus called the Gospel in order to continue his evangelical tour. It's possible he took a position explained by Schopenhauer and would probably argue that the sight of Jesus on the cross would give strength to the compassion of ending the persecution of an innocent man. An example for people to witness so as not to follow in the same path or more perhaps to witness the consequences as a result of your moral compass pointing in the wrong direction.

Christianity welcomes those who are contrite and broken hearted. Nietzsche on the other hand, saw pity as a weakness and harmful to life causing depression and loss of strength. He likened it to a sickness that should take its course and have those naturally perish or be destroyed. He welcomed this resolution and offered to help, asserting that any vice is harmful and practical sympathy is Christianity. He felt Christianity denies all reality, turns truth into lies and creates distress to make itself immortal. He believed man's instincts sustain growth and development and states that where the "will" to attain power is lacking, there is decline. He placed an importance on instinct, being the basis for which consciousness and spirit are derived.

He further states that human "will" is reactionary and is only present with a stimulus.

He considered "life" itself the instinct for growth, for durability, for accumulation of forces, for power. This describes somewhat of a military threat or invasion or the moment of facing death, similar to the reaction experienced when confronting a wounded tiger or bear.

My own experience had to do with fasting. I had never "fasted" until I started attending church services at The Church of Jesus Christ of Latter-Day Saints. The way it was explained to me, the purpose was to invoke the Holy Spirit, present a stimulus, and to become conscious of the reaction.

It is hard for me to understand the foundation of how the spirit is derived, although Nietzsche's point is valid when delving in the study of AI and machines becoming sentient.

Frederich Nietzsche feels mankind is corrupt, void of instincts and self-destructive, preferring what is harmful or "nihilistic", meaning that the harmful nature of being a protector or savior increases confidence to be forgiven. This in turn invites decadence, and eventually leads to man's extinction with a tendency to destroy life.

Nietzsche despised Christianity as a religion of peace since he felt that Christianity depraves a man of core instinctive values, making "nihilistic values dominate under the holiest names".

He doesn't believe Christianity is real because he felt it is based on fiction and lies and purports a hatred to nature and anything natural. He saw Christians as weak and in order to become strong and confident, they should adopt a God who is good and destructive, similar to the traits of Apollo.

He further stated that to counter decadence and a state of hopelessness, they should alter their concept of God to one that loves friend and foe alike, since a God that does all good, that hates nature, and opposes the will to live, attacking anything "present day," relies on lies about what is coming in the future and the great "beyond".

Anything evil tends to be attributed to a higher power, he stated. Nietzsche questioned what was being deified. He felt that this concept was a contradiction of life and is valid compared to The Gospel as evangelized by the Apostle Paul which essentially makes a celebration of a person's death. According to Frederich Nietzsche, the Jewish church opposed and negated nature, reality, and the world as being sinful and unholy. Christianity then rejected the Jewish church and its holy, chosen people. Frederich Nietzsche is a known atheist and rumored to be homosexual. Since he did not believe in God, he couldn't understand the meaning of God's "will".

Leadership can be defined as action, knowledge, philosophy, and growth in a person. By using examples from biographies and an author's personal life, we discover effective strategies that help leaders solve problems, make choices, and inspire people. Mentorship, which was demonstrated by Aristotle who mentored Alexander the Great, is the foundational pillar for developing capable and visionary leaders. Fundamentally, Aristotle offers some insight on the type of tools that leaders have at their disposal.

His understanding of "tragedy" as a process which purges the soul provides the reader with a critical approach to the emotional state of one's character. Managers and leaders always have loads on their shoulders and the capacity to transform challenges into something manageable in an environment of humility is cathartic, according to Aristotle.

Mentorship plays a central role in leadership development. Alexander the Great is a product Aristotle's teachings at Plato's Academy where he developed military training and strategic skills. This kind of mentorship shows the importance of transferring knowledge and promoting development to the brightest scholars. Forging strong ties with role models allows potential leaders to grow in character and are encouraged to help others grow as well.

There is a tendency to focus on what a leader lacks or the quality of his/her performance in order to build and improve traits needed to lead others. Humility becomes a part of you and serves as a tool of change since leaders who possess such character transform, and are able to relate to people more directly. Other insights are derived from Arthur Schopenhauer's philosophical ideas and perspectives from Frederich Nietzsche.

Pity was the highest virtue according to Schopenhauer, exemplified with methods using empathy and compassion. Empathy as a leadership approach can help to create trusting relationships and motivate people.

In contrast, Nietzsche refuted this concept and regarded pity as a vice and felt that the 'Will to power" is the use of a powerful source of strength, which supports endurance and determination to get motivated. These views can be integrated by leaders, fostering the virtues of being compassionate in order to handle complex endeavors.

Following Nietzsche's concept on instinct and the reaction to stimuli, the demand of decision-making calls for leadership under intense pressure.

Culturally, practices like fasting as of the Church of Jesus Christ of Latter-Day Saints offers a unique instrumentality to leaders. It allows people to embrace frugality, discipline, hard work, and perseverance all of which are very important in leadership. Some leaders may use the Holy Spirit or an increased level of awareness to align their consciousness with their goals and get direction in their decision-making. This practice highlights the need for leadership development in order to form one's thoughts and emotions carefully.

Leadership is also about confrontation of issues that put to the test one's beliefs and staying power. In general, Nietzsche's philosophy of life as the "will to grow" and attain power is the same as the "will" to persevere in leadership.

Managers encounter some decisions similar to facing a wounded tiger – circumstances which master the art of control and require swift action, courage and critical decision. All of these experiences make leaders, prepare them for upcoming challenges and change by creating drive and resistance.

Finally, through mentorship, and by taking advice from Aristotle's theological belief and philosophy, leaders can develop strength, compassion and true meaning in their lives. Humility and self-discipline are other applications to help foster growth in order to endure hardships and to prepare members of your team.

# Chapter 3:  Apocalyptic Thought and Business Legacy

A Philosopher's thoughts: Greece is known as the cradle of civilization and earlier I made reference to how mythological figures represented scenarios of life for a mortal man on earth. At some point in history, philosophical and theological thoughts crossed paths and I believe this represents our understanding of two worlds, the divine, spiritual world and the earthly, mortal world of life on earth.

I will use Apollo and Dionysus as the foundation for interpreting the views of some of the most renown philosophers. First, we have to determine if these philosophers believed in the existence of God or were known to be atheists.

Let's say that a philosopher was optimistic of his views, remained positive and believed that an abundant life of happiness could be achieved. On the other hand, another philosopher took a negative approach, all is hopeless and a final reset, end or destruction is the resolution to all of the world's problems. We have a dichotomy, two ends of the spectrum, like two poles of a magnet or the earth, north and south. Apollo is another deity known as an oracle of Delphi. It is said he was a healer, sought to ward off evil with his bow and arrows having invented archery. He was also known as Helios, a term that identifies the Sun. He became the patron of herds and crops protecting them from disease and avoiding famine.

He was known as a colonist and established laws for early civilization upon consultation with his oracles, yet he was able to bring destruction, ill-health and plagues with his arrows. He was a wrathful god. According to Greek religion and mythology, Dionysus is the god of grape-harvest, fruit orchards, vegetation and religious ecstasy.

The Romans referred to him as Bacchus because his wine, music, and ecstatic dance brought joy and celebration for those oppressed by the powerful. His followers were known to be freed from the restraints of self-consciousness, fear and care. By engaging in such "bacchanalia", his enemies opposed the freedom of expression he engaged in. Represented here are two figures in early civilization, Dionysus, celebrating life, joy and happiness, and the other, Apollo, capable of destroying that which he can create.

Philosophy itself developed when attempts were made to explain the existence of certain phenomena which cannot be explained. As studies continued, philosophers felt the need to know how the mind processes events and the sensory perception used in forming an explanation. Most philosophers feel that space and time does not exist outside of each one of us. They take a relative approach similar to the concept from the "Theory of Relativity" by Albert Einstein, and suggest that the elements associated with certain phenomena appear to us only from our senses forming intuitive thoughts from past experience much like dreams.

Although, certain spiritual phenomena can transcend what we intuitively perceive with our senses, and there is a tendency to determine its reality based on transcendentalism. This is a philosophical system known as transcendental idealism brought forth by Immanuel Kant in the 18th century. When our mind develops an explanation, it collects what occurred and makes sense of it from human intuition. In summary, since dreams are derived from what we encounter in our own experience, Immanuel Kant reveals the factor for determining its reality is what results from the use of our senses and stems from the space and time of each individual, respectively. He described space and time as real, but transcendentally "ideal". Arthur Schopenhauer was another German philosopher who adopted Kant's views and considered himself an idealist.

Frederich Nietzsche saw Schopenhauer's philosophy, as nihilistic, meaning self-destructive and opposed to life and claimed Schopenhauer supported pity as the highest virtue. Schopenhauer based morality on compassion. Schopenhauer claims that knowledge of the inner nature of the world and life results in the "perfect resignation" which essentially is the innermost spirit of Christianity. Although Schopenhauer was critical of all speculative theology brought forth by German idealists like Kant, such as transcendental, transcendent, and reason.

He felt it was an attempt to explain and bring forth views on God, free will, and immortality. Schopenhauer labelled them notions that were beyond experience, not real. Kant described these same notions as faith and belief and called Schopenhauer's "empirical world" existed only in our mind. I tend to side with Schopenhauer in claiming that our knowledge and experience of the world is direct. Schopenhauer further explains his position in *Book One of The World as Will and Representation* and went on to develop his "Theory of Colors". The time was the Age of Enlightenment or the Age of Reason. This was an intellectual and philosophical movement in Europe during the 17th and 18th century.

His investigations became most important in finding a demonstration for the "priori nature of causality." The difference between Kant and Schopenhauer is how we analyze and comprehend that which has an effect on us in terms of sensations and perception. Perception appears more related to the mind, a thought process of which Kant proposed that its content could be identified empirically. Sensation is limited to what is felt on your skin and what you perceive to lie outside of you.

Schopenhauer went on to further explain the understanding of sensations as a representation of cause and space based on experience and familiarity with those sensations. Nietzsche was able to define notions of good and evil. Good is whatever augments power, power itself.

Nietzsche believed evil stems from weakness, anything that develops from weakness, like pity, compassion and a moral aptitude. He felt "happiness" is the feeling that enables power over others.

He went on to say that it is a feeling which the status of power increases, in his logic, embracing "happiness" allows you to overcome resistance, adopting a protective state of mind. I tend to seek happiness in sports, having a favorite and following the team's outcome. My brother would tell me that a lot of people would ask him why he goes to the sports page first when he opens up a newspaper. I will always remember his response. He said, "It's because I want to read about man's victories instead of man's losses in the world."

## Long-Term Legacy vs. Short-Term Gains

In my view, the problem of choosing between a long-term perspective and short-term benefits is arguably the most important and most frequently posed question in human decision-making. This is a philosophical, theological, and, most importantly, practical question that lies at the core of both personal and communal being. The use of concepts from both, ancient mythologies, particularly the Apollonian and Dionysian archetypes, as well as the philosophical disciplines of Kant, Schopenhauer, and Nietzsche can shed light on coping and being prepared when facing the unknown.

Apollo and Dionysus are personalities. They represent two different aspects of managing life and decision-making in general. While Apollo may be viewed as the god of light, reason and prophecy, he embodies the long-term horizon, the "big picture" in other words.

The origin is from organization and the cultivation of civilization. The result shows stability, continuity, and qualification of chaos. The connection exists with healing and lawmaking (Medicine and Law), since there is evidence of long-term strategic planning from the use of destructive anger and the power of inflicting plagues with his arrows. Most long-term decisions require making hostile decisions or at least difficult decisions to achieve a notion of goodness.

In contrast, Dionysus represents wine, festivity and anarchy which are behaviors identified with short-term gains and hedonism. His domain concentrates on the raw feelings of real life, one of passion, and instinct. Dionysus is out of bounds and free spirited, and yet any society served by him is a society on the edge of the cliff, shaking in anticipation of a plunge into the abyss from the reverse side of excess.

These archetypes are not two opposites but work in parallel serving as two forces. Step by step, an Apollonian way of thinking prefers order and continuity, as well as tradition and calculation to be prepared for future obstacles. A Dionysian approach teaches us about joy, flexibility, and how to grasp what's currently available to us.

It is common in management to synchronize these forces and use the advantages each has to offer at the same time minimizing liabilities. The duality of long- and short-term strategies are typically present in the study of philosophy

It is also typical of planning and undertaking changes in your life and in business. Building a long-term legacy involves preparing for the future and the structured approach under Apollo supports this strategy emphasizing the effects on a future generation. Kant has viewed space and time as mere creations of mind, so also the legacy, what we leave behind, is therefore a creation in our mind and perception. He clearly dismisses the experience, history and tradition founded in an organization.

The equally plausible assessment can be provided by Arthur Schopenhauer.

He stands on Kant's thought but rejects speculative theology and concept of faith and stresses experience and death. His emphasis on the "will to life" is specifically Dionysian – desires are given priority over reason, so the potential for life is often prioritized ahead of time. In keeping with Schopenhauer's view about causality and perception, it must also be noted that the smaller effects are also significant in this context of doing everyday work for big goals.

Friedrich Nietzsche goes even further and breaks down morality and evil into power and energy. For Nietzsche what matters is power and self-effacement, which are indeed yardsticks of success.

This perspective can be seen as a synthesis of Apollonian and Dionysian traits: the order of Apollo with the emotion of Dionysus.

Therefore, Nietzsche's insistence on the use of confrontation and assertiveness in addition to finding joy in overcoming a task is a valuable principle to apply in preparation for the next confrontation.

## Impact on Decision-Making

The philosophy of Kant, Schopenhauer and Nietzsche offer useful insight for decision-making in regards to developing a system of permanent or long-term record or legacy or for a short-term account.

Kant's point about space and time being merely phenomenal means to imply that our decisions are preconditioned by our perceptions. This becomes useful when considering any type of selection or inclusion which requires decisions made without bias or favoritism.

How do we overcome challenges amid uncertainty? Strategies for making a decision can be placed in practice using concepts and disciplines of philosophy. By looking at the Apollonian and Dionysian archetypes and philosophies of Kant, Schopenhauer, and Nietzsche, we can come up with a strategy for decision-making that incorporates all of the available resources.

While Apollonian thoughts imply order, one presupposes efficiency and a variety of strategies based on reason. Dionysian thought exemplifies connection with emotion, and of trusting one's own instincts. When used in conjunction, there is a dynamic that plays out where reason informs instinct or instincts inform reason. As outlined above, Schopenhauer never underlines any spiritual values, rather his emphasis on "will" means that decisions should not be based on ideas but actual experience.

How do we make this decision right now, for instance, immediately or "on the fly?" According to Schopenhauer, your experience in this type of situation will inform your instincts and calculate a course of action. As a result, someone with more experience will have a more positive resolution. Kant argues that this empirical thought is only in your mind. He further made the assertion that by overcoming your instincts based on your own principles leads to making a decision and giving reason to a moral imperative. This self-directed action introduces agency to Nietzche's approach: it is the means and end of resilience. Simply, ending your efforts, cutting your losses. This usually pertains to decisions made on short-term performance (what have you done for me lately, characteristically efficient) and could potentially have a negative impact on the future.

## Strategies for Resilience and Readiness

With the help of the mythological symbols of Apollo and Dionysus as well as the contribution of Kant, Schopenhauer, and Nietzsche, I will try to uncover this conflict and look at its influence on decision-making more extensively.

In reference to Kant, the appreciation of the effect of perception on decisions will help decrease bias and improve perception, implying that our decisions are preconditioned by our perception.

Perception can be greatly influenced by a practice in Engineering called "trial and error". By reflecting on the progress of your project, you can decrease bias by studying the results from "trial and error" and quantify the experience encountered.

This is done by analysis and validation, which eventually decreases bias of the perception used to make a decision.

Here I submit my proposition of logic: Decreasing bias through validation, preconditions our perception

Here are the steps: Quantify through experience (experimentation), validate the perception, weigh bias, make a decision.

This mentality is similar to that of Dionysus –- one must be ready for changes. Where the environment is unpredictable, it's therefore appropriate to be flexible and creative in finding approaches to problem solving.

There are a number of methods and tools to use when preparing for possible obstacles that one might face.

Scenario planning or "role play" methodology is a form of study. Other experimentation methods include "stress testing" to learn certain levels of endurance. It is found that a clear sense of meaning can act as a cornerstone of purposeful resilience and these methods will reveal a pattern of priorities that inspire action. The objective is to have individuals and organizations sustain focus in the midst of trial.

Kant's writing is replete with the principle of ethical reasoning to deter people from making profitable decisions at the expense of morality. Decisions may become hasty and influenced by financial pressures or looming compliance or regulation policies.

To further enhance resilience to bad decisions, it has been found that collaboration and community support is helpful. Using multiple voices and sources provides an efficient solution to address making complicated decisions.

In relation to Nietzsche's account of power as the overcoming of resistance: it _is_ the power of collective strength. One might easily state that every difficulty and each failure is a perfect chance to learn.

What Nietzschean attitude offers people and organizations is harnessing the experience of adversity in order to spur change and growth. Training for a growth mindset lays a foundation to be resilient and ready for the future, because there are always those that are willing to keep on learning.

Tradition plays a massive role when it comes to decision making and determination to push through to the next level. It is a part of the inclination to leave a legacy and follow Apollonian aspects including order and foresight. This trait can be seen among politicians placing emphasis on creating a legacy, as opposed to the teachings of Dionysius which makes people realize that it is not only about creating a worthy memory, but also about living worthy now. In times of crisis, the party life of Dionysus gets placed on the back burner and there is more of a focus on immediate concerns or repairing critical problems.

This chapter has discussed how these perspectives relate to an organization when managing resilience and preparedness. Understanding the roles of reason and how we make decisions can help us live through the maze of contemporary society.

When we apply a philosophical view in our day-to-day existence, we can better manage acceptance of risk and regard for principles, values and posterity.

## Chapter 4:  Biblical Insights on Wealth and Stewardship

### Biblical Teachings on Wealth

The teachings of Jesus Christ help us think about caring for others in need and offers ways for those more fortunate with the distribution of wealth.  Jesus Christ always emphasized treating others as you would yourself, and presents a lesson for us to mitigate poverty and allows men of God to receive the basic necessities like food and shelter. The scriptures of Jesus's teachings about wealth are significant in today's world when we see those more fortunate spending most of their wealth on their own luxuries.  This is against the teaching of Jesus Christ which conveys the responsibility of the wealthy to feed the poor so that poverty can be eradicated from the whole world.

Webster's dictionary defines wealth as "the stock of useful goods having economic value in existence at any one time." President Ronald Reagan was admired during his term for a being a Godly individual, upholding his conservative and religious views from 1981 to 1989.  In governing the economics of this country, he championed a policy known as "trickle-down economics" which follows the same principle.  There are those that continue to defend such theories which assumes that economic growth, encouraged by a free market, will inevitably succeed in bringing about greater justice and fairness in the world.

Meanwhile, there are citizens still waiting today for opportunities to "trickle down" amongst their communities and families, placing a crude and naïve trust in the goodness of those wielding economic power and in the sacralized workings of the prevailing economic system. This changes the disposition of the whole world, sustaining a lifestyle which excludes others, as a globalization of indifference has developed.

In the world of wealth and money management, risk and return are considered big factors when business professionals work behind the scenes creating successful financial strategies to generate revenue. It is important to accumulate assets while utilizing risk management to earn a profit that consists not only of money but also of satisfaction. In a modern sense, wealth is defined as possession, amount of money, or other valuable resource which individuals or families own and enables them to live comfortably. To some of us, wealth is having a steady source of income in order to be financially stable in the short run as well as in the future. If we are not counting ourselves as rich by American standards (above or below poverty level), we are indeed wealthy by global standards, for most of us anyway. The Bible has a different concept of wealth and sets people to ponder over the proper attitude toward property and success in the context of God's kingdom.

Here in this chapter, I will provide a better understanding of prosperity including both the spiritual and physical aspect of wealth.

Its emphasis is more about having enough and being a good manager of what one has. Others define wealth pertaining to what is an "appropriate amount" of resources and property.

The understanding of wealth in biblical terms is not a matter of amassing riches and becoming rich, rather striving to have enough to live well and achieving what you were created to be in God's image. Once you have professed your faith in a higher power, further study shows it is God who gives the power to attain wealth.

In **Deuteronomy 8:18**, we get a reminder that says, *"But remember the Lord your God, for it is he who gives you the ability to produce wealth."* This recognition that God is a provider is the basis of any biblical concept of prosperity. Wealth therefore is a divine provision which supports our efforts, to the purposes of God.

There is a distinct differentiation of 'wealth' and 'riches' in the Bible. The two terms are sometimes used synonymously, although the connotation is different. There is more emphasis on the attitudes brought forth that arise from the heart of their owners. The Word of God speaks quite a lot about how wealth develops the character you portray and the spiritual state you convey. The attitude and kind of thinking prevalent today is described by the rich Ruler in **Luke 18:18-25**. When Jesus invites him to follow Him, he could not do it because his riches and possessions had become his gods.

His wealth and greed had become his eyesore and he misses out on the heavenly blessings of being a disciple of Christ, because he cannot let go of his wealth for a spiritual life.

It's hard to believe that a country in Europe ruling as an oligarchy governed over our neighboring country, Mexico.

The French Rebellion has to be one of the most significant revolutions of our time involving those masses in conflict with those of similar traits and cultural characteristics in the same country. This was a battle royale of the have's and have nots and exemplified how detrimental a society torn between two classes can be. The significance is elevated when you look toward Mexico and a society that was being transformed into an oligarchy system of rule so close to our own country, and yet traces of a stratified society still remains.

The 1921 Mexican Revolution was a rebellion of farmers and landowners against land grabbers and right to property, essentially, rightful owners protecting a land of their own and the existing threat of being taken away. It seems rebellion starts when the threat exacerbates and social classes form, always based on wanting to live a better life filled with happiness. Those that rebelled had a passion for property rights, education and healthcare. All of the important goals and elements of securing a future was taken away and with determination, they were forced to defend themselves and take it back.

John Paul II reflected on global peace on May 1, 1991, by describing a conflict which set man against man, almost like "wolves."

A conflict between the extremes of mere physical survival on the one side and opulence on the other and set his intentions to intervene with a mission to *"feed his lambs and tend his sheep"* **(cf. Jn 21:15-17)** and to *"bind and loose"* on earth for the Kingdom of Heaven **(cf. Mt 16:19).**

He intended to restore peace and the reader cannot fail to note his severe condemnation of the class struggle.

The information I was given from church members when I inquired about the purpose of a church was to the include among its essential elements, a proclamation of the Church's social doctrine. This doctrine is to become the source of unity and economic life when confronting situations and responding to the great challenges of today. We face these situations without degrading the human person's transcendent dignity, either in oneself or in one's adversaries and form a just solution.

In the days of Pope Leo XIII, this doctrine remains suitable to respond when ideologies are being increasingly discredited.

At that time, the approach to solving the problem between capitalism and labor was life or death, or was described as a two-fold approach. One directed to this world and this life, to which faith ought to remain extraneous or the other directed towards a purely other-worldly salvation, which neither enlightens nor directs existence on earth.

In 2013, Pope Francis wrote in a letter to British Prime Minister David Cameron, "The various grave economic and political challenges facing today's world require a courageous change of attitude that will restore to the end (the human person) and to the means (economics and politics) their proper place. Money and other political and economic means must serve, not rule, bearing in mind that, in a seemingly paradoxical way, free and disinterested solidarity is the key to the smooth functioning of the global economy." This is a clear distinction which must be made as part of understanding the Gospel and applying its concept for a genuine solution. Allowing money to rule impairs a moral perspective for judgement on any solution.

We have to ask ourselves, are we part of the solution or are we part of the problem. Throughout history, Latin American countries have faced economic oppression to the point that imbalance in the global economy is the norm. It is because of this oppression and the need to battle leaders carrying a mindset of colonial rule and the use of the Gospel as a solution. Since the industrial revolution, we have seen the migration of individuals from other countries seeking alternatives from oppressive methods of enterprise and avoiding a permanent state of poverty. The crucial message presented in the scripture highlights a distinct way of living and utilizing our wealth which defines our relationship with God.

In today's society, wealth should never be a hindrance and no can ever claim that anyone is hindered by wealth unless they admit they are part of the oppressive party.

Logically, if God is the owner of wealth and gives the ability to produce wealth, then wealth is not what is hindering you, because one gains wealth with proper management and wise investments.

Jesus warned of the danger of mismanagement and remaining focused in the Parable of the Sower **(Luke 8:14)**, where He explained the meaning of *"the seed that fell among thorns"* choked by *"the worries of life, the love of money and the desires for other pleasures."* This passage refers to money that is improperly gained or mismanaged under numerous distractions and gives priority to utilization without a proper moral perspective.

Nothing is certain and it is God who provides our needs. It makes us aware that wealth is not something to boast in or put our hope upon in order to be made secure. Hence, the rich are exhorted to give alms and use their money for the common cause. The word of God says that the rich should do good, feed the hungry and be generous. The rich are managers of God's grace and what they have belongs to the Lord and should be used to give hope to the needy.

The Word of God teaches us lessons on wealth and more specifically, how to handle wealth with responsibility and accountability.

Money is not the root of all evil, but the Bible tells us in **Timothy 7:6**, *"The love of money is the root of all evil,"*

Simply, to avoid being proud, greedy, and to trust in God.

Christianity teaches us as businesspeople and individuals to steward our wealth wisely for God's glory and for the good of others and for things that have eternal value. If we are willing to regard the things of this world differently, be givers instead of takers, and believe God's word, then we can know what riches are on earth and in heaven

## Stewardship vs. Ownership

Applying stewardship is nothing more than being an instrument through which to further the Lord's work on earth. The concept is to recognize that everything we possess is not our own and has been entrusted to us by God. This is based on Jesus' message on wealth, giving, and honesty since we have been given a blessing from God.

In fact, ownership and stewardship are two diametrically opposed concepts in defining one's rights with regards to resources, objects or nature. Ownership indicates complete control and power of an entity together with the legal power to use, manage or dispose over that object.

Stewardship, on the other hand, is the duty of handling resources on behalf of an owner while always having in mind that resources belong to somebody else.

As a steward you are expected to manage resources properly with an aim of adding value to other people's lives. Stewardship is the New Testament word that describes and defines what it means to be a servant before Christ.

As **Pope Francis** said, *"money and other political and economic means must serve, not rule"* and as an owner, it is possible to become a good steward by upholding virtues such as loyalty and responsibility. Stewardship follows the mission of the company as developed by the owner. Stewardship implies servitude and acknowledges an obligation to manage resources for the benefit of all shareholders or the public as stated in the mission of the company. The owner is called to oversee these earthly assets responsibly when developing a plan and overall direction of the company's purpose. We are invited to sanctify God's name by making sure that these blessings are used for the sake of others and generations to come.

## Balancing Prosperity with Generosity

Work beyond what is required, but what is not expected, "of going the second mile." Be unique and think about things that no one else would ever think to do and apply this aptitude in your daily work. Be creative.

Good companies cultivate the second-mile mind set. Jesus himself gives this principle in **Matthew 5:41** (New Testament): *"If you are sued for another's coat, give him your two tunics."*

He said that his followers should disengage from the culture so that the others can see Him. In business, we also have to disentangle ourselves so that others may notice the business more clearly. Do not micromanage.

Sadly, many businesses demand second mile performance, yet they do not provide second-mile commitment to preparing employees and implementing policies. This is always good advice–to do more than what is required from you.

*Principle 1:*

Think of others first: Use the golden rule in your relationships. Practice thoughtfulness. Customers will think of you when you think of the customers.

A helpful principle to build a business is found in **Luke 6:31**. This verse, called the "Golden Rule," says: *'In everything, do to others what you would have them do to you.'* This principle is used by some of the top businesses. Any firm that neglects its customers will have negative views by other consumers in the market.

*Principle 2:*

Each commercial venture generates profit. Profit is the revenue from the business, which every businessman receives his earnings.

As any businessperson will attest, it is often said "you don't have a business until you have profit". Many Christian leaders know that the wrong gain can be disastrous. One of the biblical principles that Christian leaders should convey is to make a profit with a mission.

Jesus asked his followers in **Mark 8:36** "What does it profit a man to gain the whole world & to "lose his own soul"? From this verse, there is a great lesson for any leader of the church to learn.

*Principle 3:*

Strategic management is one of the most important aspects of leadership and decisiveness are essential in this case. It helps to be decisive when implementing the strategies in place to uphold the company's purpose. The ability to either affirm or deny something immediately means that you have a clear understanding of your goals. Have confidence of your end product and build trust in your words. It is said, you give your words relevance, so guide your next course of action with understanding results and or consequences. You will be able to nurture relationships informing others and know they can rely on your words. This allows others to take importance into your decisions and give support when there is disagreement.

*Principle 4:*

If an owner is capable of doing a good job, who will give recognition and say, "good job?" It is only when an owner has generated enough revenue to be able to help others and then the owner may get recognized or awarded in return for generosity. Honors and rewards are given for those that serve a company for a number of years. "Well done."

Possibly the two most effective phrases in the English language. This should be the desire of every business owner and to hear these words at the end of their tale.

*Principle 5:*

The Law of sowing and reaping has been followed by many successful businesses. Simply said, "You reap what you sow" and has been tried and tested. **Corinthians 9:6** states that *"He, that hath uttered sparingly shall also reap sparingly, and he that hath uttered bountifully shall also reap bountifully." But he who sows bountifully shall also reap bountifully."* It isn't necessary to start with a great idea, just the seed will suffice, and the crops you are enjoying today were sown the previous day. Another part of the Bible tells us that we cannot sow seed that does not produce a harvest. Hence, sow liberally and look out for your reward continuously. In other words, be careful of the seed you are planting and conserve your resources for a consistent return.

*Principle 6:*

Nothing good in this world begins without a dream. It is always a great thing when people set their sights high and feel that all things are possible. Give yourself a challenge and force yourself to look at the world from a different perspective. People want to be associated with those who have big dreams as individuals, and big goals as organizations.

**Ephesians 3:20**– *"Now unto him that is able to do exceedingly above all that we ask or think, according to the power that worketh in us, unto him be honor in the church and in Christ Jesus unto all generations forever and ever. Amen."* God wants to perform signs that will surprise you. Ask God to do more than you ask or even dream in terms of achievements. Having a big vision ahead makes people notice and they will follow it. Learn to expand your thoughts and your beliefs.

*Principle 7:*

Do not spend your time constructing items that are not going to endure. Establish the right foundation for your business so it can endure the turbulent times in the market. Use sound ethical behavior in every context, every time. This is integrity. Integrity is an important element to apply from the start and will lay a solid foundation for your business. "The time is always right to do what is right." as pointed out by the great leader Martin Luther King Jr.

Lastly, there is investment, which simply means treasure. Managers are required to commit many resources throughout their tenure as a leader. For the company to deliver value, a leader has to invest in the right people, processes and systems for the organization. When businesses are invested in wisely, they are able to expand.

Introducing biblical principles into the formation of a business is not an easy task, and this calls for change of perception. This will allow you to create goals for excellence in every task.

## Integrity

The element of integrity defines the reputation of the organization. A leader in ethical decisions creates a culture and a business environment within an organization and exemplifies how the organization conducts its business with other organizations. Business organizations managed by people who have embraced corporate ethical standards are usually characterized by high standards, professionalism and employee morale to deliver on organizational goals. This ethical climate selects employees for the right job, people who would want to work in an organization that is ethical and proper, a workforce that is ethically oriented and not one that works ethically by being forced to do so.

In addition, organizational integrity is revered in the marketplace leading to the creation of a favorable image that customers, investors and partners can relate to. Today, consumers are very conscious of an organizations' ethical reputation and tends to deal with enterprises that are ethical in their conduct. Ethical behavior turns into what can be called a competitive advantage for companies known for high ethical standards and are trusted by their customers and stakeholders.

This reputation serves as a shield during tough times because stakeholders are more willing to commit their support to a company that focuses on the right thing to do.

But integrity also has an essential role to play in certain decision-making processes. Ethical leaders have a higher ability of making decisions that are in the best interest of the organization and its stakeholders. They avoid making mistakes which could give them instant results at the cost of the company in future. It also helps to maintain sustainable growth of the company's business and its objectives, making the company more ethical and responsible, which better correlates with the benefits of society.

Integrity is the basic foundation on which leadership character and organizational character or reputation is established. It is not only at the core of leadership and leadership credibility, but it also shapes the organizational culture, organizational success and sustainability.

If integrity is the guiding principle of leadership character, the reputation of the leader and the company are created side by side and from the ground up builds sustainable success forming long term trust and respect.

Integrity in leadership is simply about doing things right in a given capacity and at the same time, doing the right thing. Decision-making becomes based on ethics rather than convenience and organizational heads who adopt this principle foster transparency and truthfulness in the company.

Such characteristics construct a strong pool of trust between the leaders and their followers, which is enormously valuable in any leadership position. The foundation for any leader's success is trust, and when integrity is the constant behavioral pattern of a leader, long-term relationships with employees as well as outside stakeholders are built on this trust.

Credibility is a component of ethical activity, and for a leader, integrity is a sign of their core principles that should be maintained. Leaders need to be open to criticism and all levels of rank and leadership should be respected. This kind of respect reinforces a leader's role to guide and shows that he/she is reliable and competent to maintain order.

Leadership integrity is the ability of a leader to gain trust of the team in order to manage risk, mobilize support and encourage the right action for the benefit of the organization.

Such a leader not only prolongs his position as a manager, but becomes a person to emulate when it comes to the promotion of such ethical standards.

Therefore, what is earned by the leader is a positive brand that is linked to the aspects of respect, fairness, and responsibility.

Consistency is the essence of integrity and contributes to the definition of a leader's honorable image and should carry forward to form the foundation of its culture, how it makes decisions and how to behave effectively when interacting with its stakeholders. A mission statement can be developed based on this culture to create a framework that defines the organization.

The mission statement will reflect an organization that is trustworthy, credible and ethical with a dedication to long-term success based on mutual respect. An organization and its leaders preserving integrity respond to issues accordingly, lead people, and create a beneficial and sustainable image in a constantly evolving environment.

**Insights from Proverbs**

Business ethics are important when it comes to the sustainability and recognition of a business in any given field. As Proverbs 11:3 notes, *"The integrity of the upright shall lead them."*

This message suggests that when businessmen and women maintain ethics in his or her enterprise, then society will associate the businessman with trust and integrity and in turn, gains customer and employee trust. Integrity in operations does have a positive impact on the ethical reputation of the company, which forms a good base for long term relations with stakeholders. In addition, creating an organizational culture that helps to meet the standards of fairness and respect encourages employees to feel valuable in the workplace, creating a team spirit that enhances productivity.

Further, faith-based businesses are more likely to have general generosity and service.

**Acts 20**: This is a passage from the Bible that says, '*It is more blessed to give than to receive*'. This message gives incentive to business owners to leave a mark in society by contributing to the improvement of society through their business success. Charitable giving, volunteerism, and local sponsorship is a way for companies that owe themselves to faith to tailor their actions in ways other than for financial gain. As the world has woken up to the realization that there is a need to provide a model of how a business should operate in compliance with the word of God, it is found that positive change can also impact the process of making a profit.

In discussing the meaning of wealth and managing its distribution, there is a need to find a general consensus of business management.

The approach would be to evaluate the best business practice using biblical teaching to support a more moralistic view.

Throughout history, church doctrine has battled with the structure and purpose of a business. There has always been conflict over how a business should comply with the word of God to carry out its operation. Of course, there are businesses that were formed early on that had nothing to do with complying to any order for discipline.

One basic theme should remain. *"Money and other political and economic means must serve, not rule, bearing in mind that, in a seemingly paradoxical way, free and disinterested solidarity is the key to the smooth functioning of the global economy."* --- **Pope Francis**

**Proverbs 31:10–31**, Exemplifies wisdom as depicted by a godly, business leader as well as the practices used which leads to profitability and kingdom productivity. Also, the synthesis of the themes found in this passage makes reference to modern scientific business research and outlines a comprehensive business model as well as a compilation of wisdom literature.

The wisdom literature in the Hebrew scripture becomes extremely useful and is a call of duty to the reader to respect God as well as man giving importance to real life experiences and events requiring deliberation and resolution.

The teachings of Jesus Christ include an underlying theme when Jesus was asked by a lawyer "Which commandment of the law is the greatest?" His response is found in **Mathew 22:35-40** *"You shall love the Lord your God with all your heart, and with all your soul, and with all your mind".*

Phronesis, or practical wisdom in English, is one of the intellectual virtues aimed at a kind of correct deliberation about what is good and what is bad for a person. Aristotle was known to have describe ways of deliberating on what actually is a right way, or recognizing what the right means towards it, depending on your moral aptitude.

In review of Hebrew wisdom literature, and the crowning achievement of Ancient Near East wisdom literature, proverbs define wisdom in terms of behavior. Through the study of behavior, the wisdom of Hebrew's literature is an achievement.

Old Testament of the Bible under the narratives **of King Solomon** proclaims, "*I have made a covenant with my eyes not to gaze at everything that I see; for whoever keeps the command is pure in heart.*" He is aware that not all can adhere to the Ten Commandments, and by making those aware that they have sinned according to the law, fair judgement will be made and pardoned. Jealousy is a negative attitude toward another person formed from a hardened heart. In reality, it's seeing what others have that you yourself don't have, distracting your self-esteem of what you are worth. This is overcome by not gazing (examining) at what you see. With your own heart examine your own worth and human dignity.

The examples reveal a sort of procedure or SOP (standard operating procedure) in the order to love and fear God, demonstrating the way to the ultimate goals you have set in your life. Practical application can be derived from character qualities you develop from righteousness and corresponding behaviors. These characteristics should flow into your work and are presented as being diligent in your work, or helping those in need.

Similarly, as King David looked towards God as the leader of Israel, those in business need to continually reorient towards the Creator.

This is consistent with the manner in which King David vehemently pursued a path in search of favor in God's heart. This orientation gives understanding of righteous (or ethical) conduct, wisdom, right relationship with God, and the kingdom of heaven. This is the will of God.

## Chapter 5:  Profit vs. Purpose

As you start a business, it is advised to develop a business plan and later manage the business operation with strategies and processes to increase revenue and profits. The objective is to cover the cost of business operations and not to decrease revenue or kill your profits.  The company's top management like CEOs or owners work on projects concentrated on high Return on Investment. The aim is to perform within benchmarks and ratios to justify profits well-beyond the investment.  Once achieved, reports will show the company's value in the market for long-term sustainability.

Generally, advisors say that the main goal is turn a profit. When we study economics, the system that drives commerce is supply and demand.  If you are selling a product or service, the ideal environment is where there is demand.  As demand gets greater, the competitive market dictates a price for your product or service.  The business itself adopts a function of survival to remain in operation by covering the cost of doing business.  The message I am conveying is the conflict over how a business should comply with the word of God to carry out the operation.

There is a distinction between its function and the purpose of the business.  There are challenges to appreciate when making this distinction and the attempt to integrate business ethics. A business can be autonomous although we still have people involved to carry out its function in today's society.

The bible provides guiding principles for this evaluation: Covenant and Justice. In its basic form, Covenant defines the bilateral relationships business organizations have with their clientele, workforce and society in general.

In this regard, the business is in a Covenant relationship with its stakeholders, the customers who expect the organization to deliver goods and services that suit their needs. The utilitarian principles of Justice state, "In business, merit should be given to both the consumers, the buyer and seller, and to the "regulators" or Governance of the company when discussing fair employee and labor relations, environmental issues, social issues and corporate governance. In this framework, businesses are expected to maintain practices for the company and its financial gain while also making sure that everyone within the company and stakeholders are protected.

It ties in with the ethical issues of labor and capital in a very significant manner. The famous economic philosopher, Karl Marx, pointed out that business owners' profit from surplus value produced by labor but do not compensate the workers. It is therefore shocking that while Marx focused on the ability of the workers to transform the social relationship of labor, he did not consider how capital creates values too. Profit is not a function of the effort of the employee but the efficiency of capital to work hand in hand with the employee.

Back in history there was a time where this challenge existed as executives earned profits more from labor than the commodity being sold. An established firm's most valuable asset were the people responsible for production, delivery and hard labor.

When business went into survival mode the labor force became the focus for reducing costs. Some workers were released, others worked without pay, others worked under undignified conditions and suffered humiliation.

Revenue is the life blood of a business and is relevant to make a profit, but not at the expense of human dignity. Workers began dying after a system imposed a mentality of "profit at any price," a pursuit of "money rules." Pope Francis felt the urgency to intervene in 2015, although this was occurring even earlier when Communism was more prominent in the world. There was rebellion and conflict, and as a result, humanity became reduced to the working class, and the wealthy.

When the Gospel was introduced to business, it was integrated in a way to justify the suffering and sacrifice to the firm. A business in operation with the intent of generating "profits only" results in the powerful feeding upon the powerless. People end up without possibilities, without any means of escape. Human beings are themselves considered consumer goods to be used and then discarded.

This isn't about the "exploited" but the outcast, the "leftovers". Profit at any price describes an operation without purpose. Just like the body requires blood to survive, a business must survive by making a profit.

There has to be a disassociation between the two, and this is where the distinction between "purpose" and "function" becomes so important:

While the functional role of the business is to generate profit, its mission is to provide value that will benefit not only the business, but society as a whole. A business is required to be accountable for paying labor as well as for proper capital management, which means resources must be used according to the mission and vision of the business.

Companies have a purpose to generate value and be useful to the world, and profit is there to help companies achieve their purpose. Working with an understanding of Justice, Covenant, and the common good, a business is capable of sustaining a 'bottom line' as well as distributing wealth to shareholders. This balance makes it possible for businesses to practice ethics and faithfulness while in the marketplace.

This also applies to a non-profit organization which should devote all of its understanding to the principles of Covenant and Justice.

**Navigating Conflicts**

This means there is a need for an organization to consider the performance of their operations and their decisions in terms of the economic gains and losses registered, revealing the effects which society receives from the operation, and whether those decisions are ethically sound or not.

CEOs in any large company have the responsibility of determining and articulating the company's financial objectives that form the basis of their business vision and plan. These goals tend to be determined by the shareholders' expectations that control decisions through market value of stocks if a publicly traded company, or if not, financial stability.

On the other hand, values, leadership and political beliefs of the CEO, together with the shareholders' demands, predetermine the organization's financial goals in nature and governance of its business strategy. This alignment of corporate objectives and leadership beliefs invariably results in major intrapersonal clashes, especially when various leaders of the organization hold dissimilar concepts of corporate success.

A new line of thought is that business must grow to sustain this position in the market. In a mature product line, growth ceases to be a function of innovation but more of a function of market share and size of operations. The argument appears to stem from the implementation of an older style of management vs. a more modern style of management.

The argument is simple: In order to avoid diminishing the prospects of a deep and robust ROI (return on investment) there must be a priority on growth, thinking that with higher growth, a greater ROI is achieved. Some CEOs argue that focusing on ROI alone could support continued success for the company. What exists are two diametrically opposed views to manage the same objective, liberal and conservative.

This collision in management style is an excellent example of a conflict between two distinct business approaches.

The objective is to generate a sustainable and scalable value for the company. The focus on ROI embodies more of a conservative view which values prudency and performance. The focus on revenue represents a bolder orientation that elevates growth and market share as the primary means to generate sustainable value. It also represents a more assertive, proactive attitude to business. Such conflicts are often manifest at different organizational levels and they are common in organizations that have grown to a stage where different generations of leaders are in operation.

There is an age gap among CEOs and age becomes a factor since older CEOs possess a more conservative attitude to business development, and may consider the idea of rapid growth as unprofitable and too risky. The newer leader in this example may consider steady growth as important in ensuring that the organization is ready to compete in a world that is gradually shifting to high velocity. Therefore, the solution is to find the right balance between these two models, where the company is on the one hand, financially healthy and, on the other – ready for development.

Managing these conflicts calls for effective leadership and understanding of the industry. CEOs have to understand which financial goals will be adjusted depending on the market situation and how it is to be best explained to the various stakeholders.

Long-term organizational vision and mission statements on the one hand, together with short-term company goals and objectives on the other cannot be compromised in shaping the firm's strategic direction for sustainable business.

## Case Studies – Businesses finding purpose

More recently, however, we have seen the rise of so-called 'conscious' or 'missions-based' enterprises as the dominant force within the economy. These brands engage in operations with an expressed social or environmental cause by addressing societal, environmental and consumer welfare issues. When these organizations integrate their organizational values and their business strategies, they gain the confidence of customers who are shopping with their conscience more than ever before. Here are examples of popular businesses with an enhanced mission to leave an imprint on both business and society.

### Patagonia: A Commitment to the Planet

This company has shown to establish a strategic purpose. This company sells high end outdoor equipment and has been conscious of environmental issues from the onset.

Later in the year 2022, Patagonia raised the bar for climate-care when its founder, Yvon Chouinard decided to sell the company to a trust and a non-profit organization so that all the profits generated would go directly to the preservation of environment.

This is a rather daring decision that stems from the company's willingness to assign its business to the purpose of creating a positive impact in peoples' lives and society rather than for profit making. Sustainability, minimalism and environmental activism are not new concepts for Patagonia: the company has always been known for its environmentally friendly fabrics, recycling policies and campaigns. The company also writes about the cases of environmentalism and environmental protection in its blog, which proves the company's environmental responsibility.

## The Honest Company: Safe, Eco-Friendly Consumer Goods

Founded by actress Jessica Alba in 2011, The Honest Company offers a wide range of products from baby care to household cleaning items, all of which are free from harmful chemicals and made with natural ingredients. The company's dedication to transparency is a key aspect of its mission, providing customers with detailed information about the ingredients used in its products and their sourcing practices.

The Honest Company also supports various social and environmental causes through its Honest to Goodness program, which includes initiatives such as product donations to families in need and partnerships with nonprofits.

Each of these companies illustrates how businesses with a mission can thrive by staying true to their values while meeting consumer demand.

These brands are not just focused on generating profit; they are committed to making a positive difference in the world, whether through environmental sustainability, social responsibility, or transparency in their operations. In an era where consumers are increasingly conscious of the brands they support, these companies serve as powerful examples of how businesses can be both successful and impactful.

## IKEA

IKEA is an example of a business model that shows people how a company can be profitable and at the same time have a concern about saving the planet as well. Informing customers through marketing, packaging and social media induces clients to support such efforts.

# Chapter 6: Leader Conscience

Management is not a process of commanding subordinates or reaching certain organizational objectives, it is much more about accountability, moral choices and credibility. Moral character is derived from the ability to distinguish the difference between right and wrong. In ethical decision-making, leaders do not act with materialistic or selfish goals alone, but rather those supported by moral principles.

A leader carries a conscience that plays different roles and defines his/her true character when faced with making critical decisions.

First, it helps to measure the outcome or consequences when choices are not clear cut, or there are ethical considerations or concerns.

A well-developed conscience will guide a leader to carry out what is fair and proper, regardless of what is beneficial to him or her or the organization. For instance, leaders have defied odds in history by maintaining their values and upholding the right course of action. Nelson Mandela suffered imprisonment for several years, because he could not accept the injustice of an apartheid system. His eventual presidency of South Africa was one of reconciliation and ethical leadership, proving that positive results can be achieved with a clear conscience.

Second, leaders that are conscience-driven and have come from organizations under the same kind of leadership have developed trust and are highly likely to be loyal.

Workers, shareholders and clients tend to follow leaders of action that follow through with what they say or promises being made. This display becomes meaningful and is evidence of genuine empathy and professionalism.

Third, perseverance is necessary for having a high level of conscience in your leadership role. This includes governance, where decisions are made in accordance with transparency and risk management. There are times when leaders make decisions inclined to gain short term benefits at the expense of ethics. The risk is greater when the end result of a certain decision made undermines public trust and causes significant damage.

Conscience motivated leaders know this is not how success is defined and tend to adhere to a more long-term goal aimed at sustaining success for generations. For example, taking measures to sustain the environment in order to minimize carbon emissions. This may be costly in short-term, although it is a responsibility taken for the benefit of coming generations.

Having a moral conscience prepares leaders to face a number of issues arising from the multicultural nature of today's global society. Ethical standards are impaired when companies and organizations engage in cross-border activities. Implementing the rule of law becomes difficult when managers are confronted with legal and ambiguous ethical standards.

Having a moral conscience allows leaders to develop rules that are equitable and legislation inherent to everyone. Leaders can then act as mediators to reconcile differences of all parties with respect and compassion.

**Pope John Paul II** made reference to the commandment; THOU SHALL NOT KILL. *"'Thou shalt not kill' sets a clear limit in order to safeguard the value of human life, today we also have to say 'thou shalt not' to an economy of exclusion and inequality. Such an economy kills."*

Having a positive moral compass helps to avoid decisions based on selfish gain without regard for others. This type of attitude exemplifies a rejection of ethics and a rejection of God, and develops into a state where ethics are frowned upon. Having a moral conscience is not just a virtue, but the key to being a successful leader.

## Developing a Clear Conscience

A clear conscience is cultivated and is not a gift or inborn asset bestowed by nature. For leaders, cultivating a clear conscience involves setting aside bias, favoritism, even hatred and slowly integrate moral judgement as well as the in-depth appreciation of moral judgement in relationships and leadership training. Here are ways to clear your conscience:

## 1. Self-Reflection and Awareness

The first key toward having a clear conscience is knowledge of self.

The character of leaders must be subjected to a conscious check regularly with a view to finding out where individual predilections or self-interest may distort any kind of analysis.

For instance, Gandhi stressed the need for self-purification, the ability of a person to scrutinize his actions and thoughts to conform with higher standards and employ these standards for preparation and readiness to make a confident decision. Taking a few minutes in the morning to journal, meditate or pray helps the individual's emotional compass to get set. Examples of questions to ask yourself are "Did I live today according to my set values or standards? or did my decisions pay attention to the welfare of others? Self-questioning keeps a leader honest. Leaders are able to correct themselves and their actions by first realizing when they were not acting according to their own principles.

## 2. Continuous Learning

It is quite common to find ethical issues where there is lack of information or if the information available is ambiguous. Moral decisions can be enhanced by undergoing professional development in order to improve on the ability to make moral decisions. Such learning includes studying ethical philosophies, histories of conscience in leadership, and cross-cultural perceptions. In doing so, leaders can diversify their decision-making process and enhance ethical judgment.

## 3. Seeking Feedback and Counsel

People often get a clear conscience with the help of reliable advisors and friends. It is very important for leaders to be willing to consult with people of high ethical standards.

Open dialogue can act as a reflective lens, exposing blind spots that the leader may not have seen. Ethical decision-making is not a selfish act; it deserves collaborative thinking and the ability to take ownership. Great leaders like Abraham Lincoln for instance were famous for hiring people who disagreed with them. Lincoln was a great leader, the "Team of Rivals" concept shows that people with a different background and views help to make decisions that are in line with higher moral values.

## 4. Embracing Empathy and Compassion

Compassion is the foundation that comprises a clear conscience. Leaders need to consciously step into the downstream of decisions being made and visualize the psychological and financial impact of that decision. Compassion makes decisions rational but more importantly humane. For instance, when a company is in a dilemma whether to have a downsizing or has decided to terminate employees, an empathetic leader will try to find alternatives to minimize adversity, offer support to the affected individuals, and look for a viable solution. Empathy is important when dealing with intercultural differences so as to ensure there is seamless integration.

## 5. Balancing Pragmatism with Principle

Conscience-based leadership is about principles. The fact is, leadership means being able to make perfect decisions that are ethical and real at the same time. Managers should not be overly moralistic or overly cynical – a balance must occur. Engaging a spiritual journey or building faith is useful with the objective of finding ways to work ethically, that are also realistic.

## 6. Practicing Accountability

To have a clear conscience, one needs to be willing to take responsibility. Managers must because they are agents of change and must accept accountability whenever things go wrong.

Taking ownership of a problem, reducing or resolving it completely enhances credibility and allows the individual to gain confidence. This method allows the manager to convey professionalism and credible leadership by opening up lines of communication and arbitration.

The other element of accountability is the process of putting in place measures which ensure ethical practices including adopting a code of ethical standards. Other areas of governance include forming ethics resources, methods and training on conduct and having organizational channels for dealing with ethical misconduct.

## 7. Fostering Community and Dialogue

Conscience is influenced by social contexts in the community of where we live. Being active in the community allows for proper alignment and communication. The challenge is that leaders need to be involved in dialogue with their teams, business partners, customers, and the public in discussing ethical issues. When leaders foster an environment that allows employees to raise the recognized ethical standards, productivity and morale increases.

## 8. Building Resilience Against Adversity

Evolving a clear conscience also envisages strengthening of the person against outside pressures, attacks and influence that endanger ethical standards. Everyone has personal problems, in some cases when decisions are made in accordance with your own personal, moral standards, there may be implications, including financial losses.

Leaders must be resilient to attacks on reputation, false accusations, and other personal issues and remain strong in their conviction even if it is painful to do so, or if it is politically incorrect. The capacity to sustain such loads, as Pope John Paul II has pointed out, is like bearing one's cross, that is, being strong willed and ethical characteristically.

Our conscience determines what exists in our hearts. It influences our decisions between right and wrong, good and bad.

**Empowering Leaders and Employees**

From the above analysis, it is clear that ethical leadership and spiritual health should be fostered in every enterprise. This chapter conveys that business moral and spiritual well-being is central to the formulation of a healthy and humane business environment. Ethical leadership relates to choosing business decisions that are financially advantageous and are moral, which means they accord to standards including, but not limited to equity, respect of human rights and social justice. Managers should be honest, support concepts of inclusion as opposed to exclusion or discrimination, and guarantee their companies' ethical activity.

Also, paying more attention to the spiritual well-being of employees, customers and stakeholders can contribute to the creation of a meaningful and balanced organizational climate in the workplace. Promoting and maintaining awareness and happiness, together with creating a passion for work could improve efficiency and have quality results. Spiritual health as a concept enhances intra-personal and social adjustment to better improve the mental and emotional health of employees in the organization.

It is inevitable that a business will encounter some form of enhanced globalization, whether it be with customers, transactions, logistics or expansion. An organization will seek to create a harmonious environment by placing into practice diversification within its operation. For such a culture to be developed, community-orientated approaches need to focus on care and understanding.

Leadership may find that by creating a culture of love, peace and justice as the foundation of the workplace, an increase in productivity and organizational effectiveness will be produced.

One of the most effective methods to enhance business culture is to impart ethical values with the use of stories. That is why unlike any other skill, storytelling is a universal way of getting individuals from different backgrounds to develop and foster a shared understanding. In this process, one can mention that preserving history has always been one of the primary functions of stories in a society. For example, indigenous people still talk to their children by the use of storytelling to teach them about interacting with nature, other people and the role of the culture that they have.

While these may be simple narratives that tell stories, some are light-hearted and perform significant ideological work of imagining a community and mobilizing group cohesion. At work, the use of storytelling is a technique that can assist in the development of the company's culture. When employees hear each other's stories, their customs and views, they gain an attitude of understanding and respect.

For organizations, it is important to realize that promoting love, peace, and justice is not something initiated without the support of leadership. This commitment has to become an integral part of the organization in full view, operational, and in all spheres of the organization. These values need to be reflected in their actions, decisions and behavior in reference to their employees. When leaders listen to other people and care about them, practice fairness and equality in making decisions, others are bound to follow their example everywhere.

# Chapter 7: Temptations and Trespasses in Business

To clarify this view in the modern world, I'll give an example. Having a drink to relax is still accepted in society today although you have to be a certain age to partake. The usual age is 21 and there are certain state laws that regulate selling alcohol regarding establishments and open containers in public. There are also sobriety laws against driving under the influence. Partaking of alcohol has clouded one's reasoning and thereby can be considered morally evil.

This statement is hasty but it will certainly cloud your decisions and judgement on different things such as operating a motor vehicle. It becomes very easy to lose coordination, especially hand-eye or even muscle coordination since alcohol is a depressant and tends to relax your nerves. At this point, you can assert that you may not be consciously aware that you have turned onto the wrong street or you overlooked the stop sign. Did you deliberately intend to turn on that street or pass the stop sign? Well, what happens next is that the police pulls you over and makes you aware that you passed the stop sign, and you may ask, "What stop sign?" Now that you are aware what you did was against the law, your demeanor changes, maybe sorrowful and remorseful.

When you are not under the influence every other day of your life, you follow the law and make certain decisions and believe you are aware of your surroundings. What apparently happened was that the alcohol affected not only your conscience but that of your soul also.

Your reasoning was clouded down to your soul and you passed that stop sign. Maybe it's because you are on the wrong street which you turned on earlier. What made you turn onto the wrong street? Didn't you see the street sign? You drive home every day, aware of your surroundings and location, and certainly know how to find your way home.

You begin to ask yourself, if only I hadn't made that wrong turn. What made me turn on that street? It's as if your whole conscious was somewhere else, asleep maybe? Did you give permission for your conscience to go to sleep? It's possible your conscience fell asleep because of the alcohol and a trespass occurred. You certainly wouldn't have turned on the wrong street in the right state of mind, but you did anyway. You began to realize that you did not give consent for that to happen while you were really asleep.

This cannot be called a sin committed by you since your soul's reasoning was clouded even though you will suffer the consequences of breaking the law while driving a motor vehicle. Alcohol and the consumption of alcohol becomes the sin and therefore is considered morally evil. This probably explains why the product is heavily taxed when engaging in trade.

I examine businesses today and see the massive amounts of revenue being generated, and I wonder how did these entities develop to what they are today with sound reasoning over the soul and a clear conscience. I'm beginning to learn now why there are so many references made about selling your soul.

Aristotle believed that guilt and shame is part of the human condition as well as the different ways people cope with regrets, past memories and feelings of remorse. In a way, Greek philosophers usually described this condition in Greek mythology for instance, in the manner of coping with addictions such as alcoholism.

The healing process for such iniquity is a coping mechanism for the onset of medical ailments brought forth as a result of alcohol abuse, probably inherited from Bacchus. Prometheus is an example of a Greek mythological figure cast out for his transgressions. This was seen as punishment, with buzzards pecking at his liver throughout all eternity. This is a real process that most people can grasp and truly feel, and is used to associate the human condition with something concrete and tangible. This would surely drive more understanding on how to cope with such tragedy.

Maybe it's easier to understand because the ancient Greeks believe that humans have free "will" and like Adam are born into a fallen world.

Depravity, confinement, isolation, imprisonment, or any punishment for transgressions of known doctrine or any attempts to take away free "will" or corrupt this very nature are all considered unnecessary by Gnostics during the Reformation, asserting that man has an inherent sinful nature.

Christians opposed the assertion and writers implied that humanity has the ability to live righteously, the core of God's "will", and avoid God's future judgement.

The first Christian author to discuss the fault of sin was Justin Martyr and claims that fault lies at the hands of the individual who committed it. The early writings by Saul of Tarsus, later to be named Paul, suggest that he too believed individual human responsibility for acts of sin. Paul also wrote mostly about receiving the Holy Spirit and John introduced baptism as the channel to receive the Holy Spirit.

The story of Paul of Taurus is fascinating. He persecuted Christians for following Jesus and practicing Christianity. The apostle Paul was said to be a member of the Sanhedrin, a Jewish judicial body that carried out atrocities against Christians. Jesus was tried before the Sanhedrin after he was arrested in Jerusalem.

Earlier in life, Paul was arrested, thrown in jail and experienced a miracle performed by the power of God when the prison crumbled to the ground and he escaped. I believe Paul was wrought with fear.

He feared not having what he preached about. Faith. In the belief that he would not experience life after death and tried hard to avoid it. He had to come to terms with the realization that he had become a part of the very system he opposed and took part in, resulting in the murder of Jesus Christ.

I believe this is the point of his conversion and the belief that he could live a life on earth as it is in heaven. Here is a story on miracles which applies to Paul's thought process:

[There was once a rich man who asked a saint (Santa Vivent) for a miracle to strengthen his belief. At that moment, a group of peasants gathered in his presence and behold, gold coins appeared in their hands. The rich man turned to the saint and said, *"No, this is not sufficient for me to believe."*

At that moment, the gold coins filled his hands and the rich man was now satisfied and is now a believer. The rich man could not believe after the first miracle because he didn't care about those around or in proximity to him. He could only believe when a miracle involved himself].

A life in heaven filled with shame and guilt, sorrowful for the heinous actions he had taken and the burden of the cross he was made to carry. Here is a testament of Paul's Faith in God:

### Acts 16:25-26 King James Version (KJV)

*"And at midnight Paul and Silas prayed, and sang praises unto God: and the prisoners heard them. And suddenly there was a great earthquake, so that the foundations of the prison were shaken: and immediately all the doors were opened, and every one's bands were loosed."*

--------------------------------------------------------

Unethical 'encroachment' in business does not just happen but is the result of bad decisions and mismanagement. In openly competitive markets, there are pervasive financial constraints, and critical decision-making criteria, forcing people and institutions to behave unethically.

This is prevalent not just within company's operation, but also just the mere participation and entry into the competitive market.

You will encounter those that wish to discredit your organization or make accusations that simply are not true. Implementing ethical standards starts by establishing a set of guidelines as a foundation from which leaders and organizations are going to follow. This framework should extend from the culture of the company with hard and fast rules that start with a code of ethics.

The type of code that is valuable to the organization starts with simple manners. Supplements to these ethical standards include training, workshops and, most importantly, the actual demonstration of the guidelines in practice by the managers and the leaders of the organization. By placing so-called 'key people' to manage this process, and integrate proper elements of the subject such as practical defenses, transparency and auditing.

Practices can tie into aspects of integrity by discovering areas of improvement, review and costing of financial processes, or reporting of suspected and probable conflicts of interest.

Ensuring that the communication channels are open is as vital as the foundation that enables it. This means that employees must be encouraged to report issues that they find either unethical, suspicious or unclear. Transparency and accountability are management styles implemented by leaders with a clear conscience. The result is a company culture that embraces inventiveness, teamwork and perseverance. People then begin to value the worth of their contribution.

Training can be offered in preventing misconduct and displaying responsibility in addition to two important measures which stresses the importance of protecting whistleblowers and anonymous reports.

Managers can transfer an understanding of prevention strategies. An example is developing a system of checks and balances where managerial decision-making is structured with people performing checks and balances to inhibit one person from making decisions that are unethical.

These measures of workplace ethics do not always work, and ethical transgressions are sometimes committed intentionally or unintentionally and have had damaging results. Several organizations have suffered severe consequences and lost their reputation, image and integrity. This reduces the company's stability, and undermines shareholders' relationships.

Records show that many firms have been brought to their knees by unethical behavior in the past.

Law and government agencies often enforce wrongdoing in a business environment and publicly declare that a business has engaged in an unlawful or unethical activity. The business is then subject to financial penalties which could prove devastating. Other corrective measures taken would be to address any damages, pain and suffering caused by the activity. This may involve money compensation, changes in policies, or putting resources in reparative actions.

For instance, a firm that was convicted to have caused pollution of the environment has to ensure it starts promoting environmental conservation and also spend time and resources to rehabilitate the affected region.

It is crucial and not easy to regain public trust when and if ethical breaches occur and there is a need to be transparent during this phase. The implementation of reform has created the need for organizations to provide information on their progress of reform goals to stakeholders. This kind of honesty helps to develop trust and sincerity to follow through toward completing a transformation of the existing system.

Organizations should widely implement ethics training for its employees so that employees are in a better position to handle future issues. Management can show that the company is changing for the better and remain engaged in the process of regaining people's trust. Trust is built slowly and stakeholders expect companies to sustain their commitment to ethically acceptable behavior.

There is power in restoring relationships even if with those who are offended. As with the Apostle Paul, he was able to use that power with a new focus on the future. Creating actions and plans within a company must align with ethical consideration and vision. Social interaction can reverse a negative image caused by the firm. The company's reputation can be rebuilt by creating public awareness, hosting philanthropic events, and working with organizations that promote moral values. This could include reconsidering a supplier partnership, changing a marketing plan or practicing new and more inclusive recruiting.

The parable of the rich man as well as the miracle of Jesus' resurrection can teach a powerful lesson of forgiveness even in the face of resentment. The rich man could only trust in his own faith when the miracle was done on him. In the same way, it requires more than symbolism to prove that companies are serious and genuinely working for real change that will be felt and appreciated by the stakeholders involved. That is how genuine and substantive actions have to be in order to restore trust on some level. The companies which manage to succeed in restoring or upholding their credibility become more resilient since they have to restore public trust and renew organizational values.

Adhering to the code of ethics in your business is undoubtedly difficult in today's world, not to mention the growing interest of various businesses.

It seems that some businesses operate without regard to ethics inasmuch as principles can be violated, but the benefits of following ethical standards largely outweigh the potential losses. Ethical organizations do make profits and at the same time garner appreciation and faith of the stakeholders so as to sustain the organization. By being prepared, confident and taking ownership to resolve problems with compassion, a business can learn to chart its course in a pre-oligarchical world of commerce and not lose one's soul in the process.

Recalling the change which occurred in the life of Paul and his very own experience of which he gained the calling and faith, it is possible to note that businesses also have the possibility of redemption by continuing to pursue the aim of ethical integrity in the modern world.

When redemptive business practices are applied to business, perceptions and goals are formed based on attaining an optimal state of welfare, and the aim is to achieve satisfaction or accomplishment.

Development of ideas and strategies can offer a different perspective although the nature of activities usually remain focused on remediation. It is a concept of saving a company, turning things around and making it better. Such a mentality seeks to consider activities as part of a larger, greater mission with long-term goals which include ethical obligations directed toward having an impact on the stakeholder's prosperity.

Contrary to the short-term, self-interested, and egoistic motivation, this approach is based on the generation of positive outcomes, distinguishing and maintaining and actually reinforcing positive values essential for developing an organizational culture as well as the long-term welfare of all stakeholders.

It can also have an impact on the ways in which business strategies are developed and deployed. Essentially, the system that arises from salvation-oriented thinking requires businesses to function in an ethical manner, be sustainable and have a purpose.

# Examples of Redemptive Business Practices

Financial fraud cases will cause a huge blow on the company brand. The loss of trust is damaging and the time to rebuild may take a decade or even longer. The consequences have an impact on management decisions, time and effort for employees, investors, and the image projected to the community. In addition, unethical behavior erodes positive organizational culture for instance, changes in employee commitment, an increase in turnover and interpersonal conflicts. A business that is in this situation must arise and function in an ethical manner, be sustainable and have a purpose with strategies that are ethically inspired, conserve the environment, and contribute to the welfare of the community.

A good example of remedial operational strategy includes developing actions that not only serve the purpose of helping an organization accomplish specific objectives, but also ensuring that such objectives are accomplished while respecting virtues like fairness and equity as well as the environment. For these strategies to be effective, such values have to be incorporated in the overall management of these companies.

Some businesses may integrate religion as part of their objective and the focus of strategies will center on customer satisfaction needs, not only from product or service delivery perspectives, but from the influence of their products to customers. These businesses embed the customers' needs into their operations while providing value that meets their ethical goals.

This may be through providing better and more sustainable products, enhancing and increasing the quality of the customer experience or providing astounding customer services.

Many Scholars pointed out that "forgiveness" has changed greatly over the last several decades in both an interpersonal and social level. Companies that have a "forgiving" spirit have to determine where support is needed the most and become aware that to move forward from any wrongs that have been committed, all stakeholders must be enabled to involve a broader community directed toward social responsibility. Some companies have repaired wrongs from the past such as unfairness, injustices and have implemented practices aimed at restoration and reparations.

Business operational strategies are usually decision-making frameworks that indicate how resources, time and effort will be applied in the execution of organizational goals.

The same strategies are likely to be more sustainable and ethically inspired when the system is influenced by a salvation-oriented belief. For instance, a company may use operation techniques to reduce the extent of its effects on the environment, promote employment equity by avoiding nepotism and cronyism and diversify staffing by adhering to non-discriminatory practices in the workplace or more importantly, contributing to the welfare of the community.

Whereas operational strategies might be short-term oriented, a "redemptive" thought process is long-term oriented.

An organization that follows this strategy gives its funds to practices that will continue to create value over time including sourcing for sustainable materials, practicing for environmental conservation and engaging in fair trade.

It helps the business organization to meet its profit-making goals and creates a sense of ownership among the environmental and societal structures.

Salvation-oriented thinking helps businesses to see their employees not only as employees, but as significant factors within the company's goals and objectives. When employees work in a supportive and development environment, organizations are bound to record high performance, reduced absenteeism compared to other companies, and experience fewer turnover rates.

Such religious businesses are obsessed with satisfaction needs, not only from product or service delivery perspectives, but from the influence of their products to customers. These businesses embed the customers' needs into their operations while providing value that meets their ethical goals.

This is achieved by providing better and more sustainable products, enhancing and increasing the quality of the customer experience, or providing overwhelming customer service.

Patagonia is one such organization that actively practices forgiveness. This outdoor clothing firm aims at healing its relationship with stakeholders, as well as the environment.

Patagonia is commendable in its corporate policy regarding the company's main values of fairness and communal benefit. The company has a strong policy of responsibility embracing not only the products it produces but also the influence of responsibility directed toward social problems and the environment.

This is evidenced by donations to various to environmental conservation and issues involving wage and labor. By treating everyone with fairness and repairing damages, Patagonia has shown forgiveness can be incorporated not only into relationships with employees but with the planet as well. They sell clothes that are popular among the younger generation and have a program which encourages people to repair their garments instead of throwing them away called the "Worn Wear" program designed to 'pardon fashion for consumption.'

An even more compelling example comes from the ice-cream manufacturer Ben & Jerry's –whose main values are fairness and community well-being. Ben & Jerry's of Vermont incorporates forgiveness and justice into its operation by supporting legislation on racial and economic justice exemplifying its socially and environmentally activist stance.

For example, the company has made efforts toward mending the society that resulted from injustice and has backed numerous initiatives such as restorative justice and the abolition of mass incarceration.

What their approach demonstrates is that a business can leverage social media not only to make money but to also to help facilitate social reconciliation and forgiveness in order to promote a more just, social order.

Currently, there are very few companies in the tech industry that have made forgiveness and fairness part of their organizational culture. One in particular is Salesforce, where employment equity, diversity, and equal opportunities have been championed at the company. It has also adopted fairness where employees are paid equally for the equal work they do and where they observe diversity policies in the workplace. Besides its own policies, Salesforce has designated programs for corporate social responsibility, such as bringing equal opportunities in technology and education to underprivileged communities. In this way, Salesforce recognizes the lack of access to technology and opportunities prior to dealing with inclusion and aims to provide a place for social recovery in continuing Salesforce.com operations.

These companies are creating examples of how corporate organizations can shift from profit maximization to becoming organizations with character by promoting and exemplifying forgiveness, fairness and other aspects of communal restoration. Forgiveness is more like remembering and acknowledging wrongdoing and using the information to engineer a better society. Directives like these prove that a future exists where companies have a role in the process of restoration and reconciliation.

Finally, eradicating ethical violations, managing their implications and reconciliation is an organic procedure. The fortitude to carry on requires the need to be proactive, responsive and having a good degree of professionalism for repairing reputational damages.

It is therefore incumbent upon the business to realize that ethical integrity is not about espousing good moral values but utilizing these values in your efforts for your business.

Everyone including customers, employees or investors expect and demand corporate honesty, fairness and accountability.

This is why companies that adhere to these principles of management foster loyalty, create a comfort zone and find a permanent place in the market. On the other hand, when they fail, costs are generally incurred with negative consequences which are irrecoverable.

In summary, it is about a pursuit of something higher. A more positive change that is profitable for the company, society, workers, consumers, and the natural world.

# Chapter 8:  Economy of Salvation

## Applications in Business Practices

Pope John Paul mentioned the "Economy of Salvation" during a speech at a conference in 1991 from his encyclical letter "Dominum et Vivificantem" where he explained how the Economy of Salvation operates.

-----------------------------------------------------

*"Blasphemy does not consist in offending against the Holy Spirit. Rather the refusal to accept the salvation which God offers to man through the Holy Spirit working through the power of the Cross. Non-forgiveness is equivalent to non-repentance. The radical refusal to be converted, refusal to come to the sources of Redemption remain always open in the economy of salvation in which the mission of the Holy Spirit is accomplished."* **---Pope John Paul II**

-----------------------------------------------------

He makes reference to repentance and the Holy Spirit and uses the power of the Cross as a resource for accepting salvation. This economic process is always open when it comes to forgiveness or repentance. Your spiritual journey will lead you down a path and you will always encounter the power of the Cross. It is a power that you will encounter when you decide to either refuse or accept salvation. It comes down to a concise point in time of your life where you find it impossible to make a sound decision on your own.

It is a leap into the unknown and some call it a "Leap of Faith". The best way I can describe it is driving down a road that splits in two ways similar to entering an airport, and the signs above each road shows "Arrivals" or "Departures".

God offers man the opportunity to redeem himself through the Holy Spirit. This takes place through the power of the Cross. To bear one's cross is to come to sources of Redemption, where you are made aware of your transgressions and bear a laden cross. The Greeks refer to this as a thorn, a reminder usually at your side with annoying pain until it is removed.

Seeking salvation from pain, incarceration, or death is something we will all face. The psychological effects of becoming aware of your own sin is manifested in shame, guilt, remorse, fear and subjective behavior. The condition continues with a refusal to be converted, a refusal to come to the sources of redemption. This is similar to an economic exchange since you will be redeemed through repentance for coming forth and changing the path you are on and following a way of life in alignment and leading towards God, or forgiving those who trespassed against you.

The Catholic faith offers relief since Jesus Christ is the symbol for salvation and the church is supposed to provide helpful resources to ease your burden based on forgiveness and compassion.

I believe that everyone attempts to pursue a life of joy and happiness even if it appears that inherently, we are inclined to pursue a different path of disobedience which allows a quick, easy and a rather successful outcome far from God's will. When we are conscience of what path we have taken, we become aware of our displaced behavior and professionals analyze this polarization as being right or wrong, good or bad or a clinical diagnosis of bipolar. This is the study of the human psyche. Psychology tends to assert that behaviors are genealogical and ancient philosophers presented their views on this subject.

Pope John Paul II broke this down to its simplest form and individualized what it means internally to forgive and to repent.

Both forgiveness and repentance originate internally from you, an individual, and how your conscience manages its own process.

It is for your own sake, not for the sake of others to find relief from what is causing conflict with your conscience. Your mind is focused on the consequences which will arise for each decision made and is struggling to remain correct. You can be redeemed from your own attempts to forgive a person or from the guilt you carry when you take part in the economy of salvation.

Like the Apostle Paul, converting your way of thinking that is morally acceptable. To bear one's cross is to come to the sources of Redemption, becoming aware of your transgressions and to bear a laden cross.

This is the cross that constantly occupies your very existence, trying to figure out how to cope with the anguish to forgive or how be released from your guilt and shame. "The sources of Redemption remain always open in the economy of salvation" and this includes guidance on how to forgive others as well as coming to terms with the truth. John writes about salvation in **John 8:32** *"And ye shall know the truth, and the truth shall make you free."*

General practice in Catholicism is to confess your sins to a priest which in turn allows you to partake in the Eucharist signifying your acceptance of Jesus Christ in your life. If you miss the attendance of a Sunday mass, you may not be allowed to partake unless you start over again by confessing your sins to a priest.

This is the manner of converting to a different way of life, by showing your devotion and faith every week. This describes the process involved in approaching one of the sources of Redemption and finding ways to ease your burden. These are two extreme psychological conditions you will battle in your life and to find relief or redemption, there is one resource that always remains open to you. The reference to an economic process is valid. The exchange that takes place is accepting to change the path you are on. My example shows a road that splits in two and it is as if you relinquish control of the wheel into the unknown. The result is an inherent trust that you will be guided in the right direction.

When you examine these results in your life, you will find there are gains and there are losses. Let's use the simplest formula in business as the theme and describe its application. (Profit = Revenue – Cost)

Looking back, if over your lifetime you have had more losses than gains, have overall been wrought with loss, lack of revenue or resources, then this transformation in your life has been a negative experience and it is considered costly.

Conversely, if your transformation in life included increases in revenue and profits, your experience has been positive, meaning that the cost to you was covered by an increase in blessings and prosperity.

In some cases, greater costs were experienced because I sought out trust in other people, to deliver results that never transpired. I didn't bring that trust inward to myself, to trust my own judgement and discernment. Maybe because of devaluation early in life and vulnerable consequences. As a result, the guidance I needed was never attained and I failed to trust my assessment of something that is simply not true. In this case, you develop barriers and issues in processing trust in others.

If the belief in promises, betterment and prosperity never come to fruition, then the victimization continues over the years and your awareness becomes evident that a scam, trick or "trespass" has taken place.

I had made decisions on my own before in my life and I needed to fall back on my previous experience by building up my self-confidence and placing trust in myself. It becomes difficult when you receive more blessings at a younger age, and then find out the amount of discernment you must take when you seek out these so-called sources of Redemption.

The cost appears to be distrusting others, rejection, lack of opportunity and revenue, glass ceilings and facing on-going judgement. Though not my intention, making a choice to change your religion is difficult in itself, much more than just trying to learn about a different religion or denomination of which you were not raised in.

I was finally confirmed into the Catholic faith in the year 2000 and I did it to honor my parents. The loss I have experienced so far, did not develop until I accepted invitations from other non-Catholic churches in 1996. A few years before, I approached government resources available to help me get started. I never received the start-up funds and assistance which I was promised from the City of Austin to start a business.

Since I was open to learning about how religion interacts with society, politics and human psyche, I began my spiritual journey and began learning more about Christian-Protestant ideology and religion. In 1990, I accepted an invitation from a Pentecostal church as part of my journey. Looking back, I can only describe it as similar to wolves welcoming the lamb to sit at the table for dinner.

I have to be strong to overcome a victim mentality because this type of vulnerability is desirable to those wanting to take advantage. The way it turned out, it felt like my father and I were the dinner. When I was encouraged to get baptized by The Church of Jesus Christ Latter Day Saints in 2020, a number of claims were made about how my life would change, how blessings would increase in return for my donations with multiple receipts of abundance and prosperity and it all sounded very appealing. My objective going forward is to reduce costs, remain positive and translate the whole experience into increased revenue and higher profits.

## Chapter 9: Mission of the Holy Spirit in Business

## Spiritual Discernment

How does one know if a spirit is holy? The meaning of the Holy Spirit describes being Holy as being set apart from others. Spirits are all around us, they inhabit this earth. When one receives the Holy Spirit, it is assumed that the spirit is derived from the righteous framework and divine nature of God. I have just described true acts of human will which occur in God's favor and not influenced by evil tendencies. In contrast, human acts to be the result of clouded judgment or the absence of consciousness are referred to as sin. I call it non-consensual acts involving a spirit, a "trespass", as from The Lord's Prayer, "...Forgive us our trespasses as we forgive those who trespass against us." I have commented that we are all sinners, alluding to not being able to adhere to the "The Law" brought forth by Moses in the Old Testament. After studying what is known as Original Sin, I found it starts with the story of Adam and Eve in the bible.

I sought the meaning of man's "Fall" from grace, and as I tried to interpret *The Book of Genesis*, and I found further understanding by treating *Genesis* as allegory. This is somewhat in alignment with Methodius of Olympus and his understanding of *Genesis*, as an allegory, although rejecting the pre-existence of the soul in the process.

The doctrine of original sin was rejected by Clement of Alexandria focusing on the existence or pre-existence of the soul and a predisposed nature of committing sin.

In the Book of **Job 1:21**, Job refutes the idea of original sin stating the *"innocent nature"* of a newborn being born naked from the mother's womb. On the other hand, Origen of Alexandria accepted the pre-existence of a soul, predisposed to committing sin based on past, pre-world existence. It is said Adam was created by God from the earth, like clay from the ground and was molded.

Since mortality is referred to as a "being" living on this earth, we refer to man as fallen from "grace." Adam was fallen from the start having been produced by clay from the earth and then together with Eve committed acts of disobedience. The command was given by God to not partake of the fruit from the "tree of knowledge". Literally, it seems the allegory made with the "tree of knowledge" refers to gaining further understanding of science and physics which was later used by priests as a way to rule and intervene. Augustine of Hippo held that "free will" was already present in Adam as human nature, and his disobedience weakened freedom of "will", recreating human nature through reproduction and passing down this human nature to his descendants and all its hurtful desires. Augustine believed "libido" to be present in human nature before Eden or paradise, and was further transpired by Adam and Eve's disobedience and passed down by procreation.

If this is true, then Adam and Eve were not consciously aware that a sin was being committed until they were actually made aware.

Augustine believed all humans inherit the guilt of Adam and further asserted that a wounded nature is present in the soul and body of the infant and is eternally damned at birth. He later adopted a view of having no "free will" other that than the will to sin even after being baptized because of original sin.

The Church of Jesus Christ Latter Day Saints adopted this view and refers to this position in the final chapter of the Book of Mormon. The Book of Mormon states that little children are not baptized because newborns have free will and therefore God's mercy to be saved is denied. I also learned that Mormons practice baptism later in life beginning at age nine. It appears they are in accordance with Augustine, that the soul and body of the infant is eternally damned at birth and all church members adhere to the afterlife or "life everlasting." Augustine wrote "regarding those infants that have not been baptized, they entrust them to the mercy of God". I do believe in "life everlasting" although I believe that God's mercy can never be denied by anyone other than God.

The wound nature remains throughout a lifetime as a reminder to what is known as original sin and accompanying guilt associated with having disobeyed. This is what Augustine referred to as Adam's "inherited guilt" stating that an infant is eternally damned at birth and that humanity has no "free will" except to sin.

Catholics adhere to infant baptism. The Catholic church began in 33 A.D., beginning with the blood of Jesus Christ on the Cross. Jesus left the twelve disciples in charge to start a congregation with the focus to remember his presence symbolized by the rite of the Eucharist.

Throughout history, science has clashed with religion and it began when Copernicus, Kepler and Galileo demonstrated that Earth was not the center of the universe.

Their ideas were condemned by Roman Catholicism and Christian-Protestant denominations. The priests reasoned that sinners are dependent on their priests for salvation, redemption and forgiveness using "sin," "guilt," and "punishment" to oppose those attempting to become all knowing, like God.

An intervention is made with Adam and Eve and the story describes how they disobeyed, and are made aware of original sin and the need to seek redemption. The guilt process began when Adam and Eve were cast out of the Garden of Eden for their transgressions just like Prometheus.

Numerous portraits depict Adam and Eve with no clothes, being so ashamed of their bodies they found the need to cover their parts with fig leaves. Because of "free will", they were not aware of their disobedience until they aspired to be "like" God and were then consciously made aware that what they were doing was wrong. Under the grace of God initially, they were once favored by God and granted immortality. Instead, they fell from God's grace and this resulted in becoming mortal beings, just like everyone else on the earth.

We are led to believe that the end of life on earth, death, is the result of such transgressions, when really it is a natural end of one's mortality having lived upon the earth, being part "of the world" and all of its worldly passions and materialism. Nowadays, a lot of priests and preachers focus on how we live our life daily known as "Prosperity Preaching". God offers man the opportunity to redeem himself through the Holy Spirit. This takes place through the power of the Cross. Augustine felt that whatever is deemed as a "sin" is a result of clouded reasoning over the soul and is considered morally evil, but since it is not consensual, it cannot be called a sin.

Pope John Paul described bearing your own cross as repentance. The Bible doesn't describe a lot about repentance or revenge. I learned about avoiding your "heart to harden or hardening of the heart". Messages I received upon reading The Book of Mormon reflected a time in history from the late 1800's during a time when the American West was being settled. There were stories of massacres and violence most likely from conflicts with Native Americans and indigenous people of the Land, but never defining these acts of conquest for what they truly are. There is symbolism and reference to the Railroad infrastructure. I was told that one main mission at that time was to introduce Christianity to those that had never been exposed to any belief system whatsoever.

Most of the text and teaching appears to adopt principles from the way of life Jesus led and used in order to reduce violence and conflict.

I began to realize that there must have been a great amount of conflict and that this is certainly consistent with the history of conquest and oppression of indigenous people.

Imagine your own property being taken from you or burned and your family massacred and trying hard not to take revenge after being left destitute. This affects one's human condition in a number of ways and presents a lasting effect on your conscience. It would take a lot to refrain from having your heart hardened after events such as these.

I learned that the author, Joseph Smith was from New York and is considered a modern- day prophet. He was later arrested and thrown in jail probably for inciting unrest and introducing an alternative ideology which would later become a growing religious denomination. He was released from jail but was assassinated soon after he was free. This story seems to follow a pattern in history of those seeking change and improvement.

The more I think about it, he may have been restrained and confined to a mental institution. A reference in the book is made to individuals in a position of paralysis.

By paralysis, meaning unable to progress forward with any accomplishments or achievement, stoic, a life of stagnation, similar to being lost in the wilderness. It is said that this kind of person must be restrained. The restraint comes from a consensus that he is capable of unleashing some sort of threat to the establishment.

Learning more about Joseph Smith, the author's position on these matters, and the ideology in The Book of Mormon being derived from the New Testament, specifically about baptism of little children, I felt that this is not in alignment with what I had been taught.

I noticed a number of phrases with double meaning used in the language, similar to what Native Americans referred to as "speaking with a forked tongue" and a lot of contradiction with the Bible and my own ideology which I have adopted over the years. I decided to go forward with a second baptism because it was emphasized that my life would be changed.

I was in a vulnerable state at the time and invited the missionaries inside my home. They continued and pressed that I get baptized, and further said that baptism allows you to receive the Holy Spirit if you may not have received it already. So, I agreed to a second baptism as stated in my testimony and the process was fast-tracked. I was very apprehensive at the time and all I wanted to do was to learn more about what I believed in. I told them from the beginning that I was on a spiritual journey even though I was very vulnerable in my condition.

After attending a few weeks, volunteering and tithing, I was asked to be a presenter during Bible study which I enjoyed attending.

Before the year ended, I was on a fast track to elder leadership and the bishop welcomed and encouraged me to advance. I got baptized after two months and became ordained later that year. This was a new experience for me and the service was completely different.

Members would approach the altar and give testimony on what was being received in terms of baptism, spirituality, productivity and growth, and a lot of affirmation given by other members that "The book of (Mormon)" is true.

After I was baptized, I gave testimony of my experience. Here is my speech in front of the congregation:

---------------------------

"My name is Oscar J. Calderon.

I stand here today and testify that it is possible to survive without six months of coffee…I was raised Catholic.

Twenty-five years ago, I started searching for a church more fulfilling. The missionaries invited me to attend church two months ago. I felt comfortable during service and bible study and church members were very receptive. I enjoy hearing real testimony from people going through the same trials and experiences and I want to thank you for inviting me into your church.

When they asked me to get baptized, I told them I had already been baptized, but each time we met they continued to ask me. The reasoning they gave for me to baptize was to receive the Holy Spirit. I told them "No, I'm going to trust that I received the Holy Spirit when I was baptized as a baby." My apprehension was not only that I had already been baptized, but that I wholeheartedly trusted that I received the blessing of the Holy Spirit under the authority of the Catholic Church.

I was encouraged by a church member to get baptized and he told me how it changed his own life in a positive way. I asked if I was worthy to accept authority and he assured me that God will guide me. He described this authority as a true source similar to a certificate of authority in cyber security. In the cyber world, if this certificate is missing, portals are open to attack and vulnerable to hacking. I have always had faith in my belief and yes, it has been tested throughout my life in various ways and your faith will be tested also when it comes the moment of salvation and you call on authority that is not seen.

Our parents emphasize the importance of an education so that we grow in knowledge, but does this include spiritual knowledge? I began to learn more about core Christian doctrine and learned that in order to produce salvation we hope for things which are not seen, which are true and must be centered on Jesus Christ.

After attending different Christian churches over the past twenty-five years, the focus remains on the Gospel, and the price paid by one man on earth, so I accept the meaning of the cross.

I've come to accept that at this point in time, it is the intersection of a vertical line which is up and down, good and evil; and the horizontal, which is life on this earth. In ISAIAH 53:6 All we like sheep have gone astray; we have turned everyone to his own way;

This creates a burden of transgression and repentance symbolized by carrying your cross to the mount.

In Revelation, John describes the world in the last days filled with hypocrisy, lies and deception and I have prayed for strength to endure this true state of the world we live brought forth with advances in technology and biology. It becomes harder to trust our surroundings to the point of accepting published works as non-fiction when fiction or believing virtual over reality. Nephi asked if being Holy, should there be a need to be baptized? --- how much more need to be baptized if unholy.

If after being baptized and denying Jesus Christ, it was better to have not known of him at all.

So, I pray for strength.

God knows I have humbled myself before my Father. He knows the struggle to live in this world and follow the commandments as we seek perfection. No one is perfect.

As we strive for perfection, and again we seek the same authority, unseen, that allowed the birth of God's son and which we have just celebrated.

So, they informed me of a 2nd Baptism that allows entry through the gate to a straight and narrow path. An authority devoted to a mission of restoration as written in the Book of Mormon. In response to the question posed by Nicodimus if a man can be reborn, Jesus Christ said a spiritual rebirth is possible by baptism, a second baptism by water. I am now seeking to restore a lifetime of trials and tribulations, but willing to pursue a mission of restoration. I say these words in the name Jesus Christ, Amen."

----------------------------------

As you start a business, it is advised to develop a business plan and later manage the business operation with strategies and processes to increase revenue and profits. The objective is to cover the cost of business operations not to decrease revenue or kill your profits.

It is said that Jesus Christ came to pay a debt. A debt he did not owe. Businesses incur debt to keep their operation running. Some businesses are considered too big to fail (TBTF), meaning that the debt incurred by this business is carefully managed to prevent failure through reorganization or restructuring to ensure its survival. If we recall earlier, the preacher's phrase that we were bought with a price, surely this refers to our own debt that Jesus Christ paid to ensure our salvation.

We became the beneficiaries of a policy purchased to ensure that his loved ones, all people on earth were protected forever upon his death.

You may say this was an insurance policy bought from the authority of God to ensure the survival of the human race.

What does it mean when one is said to be selling his/her own soul or "he sold his soul...?" The value of your soul is determined by your own way of life. Since a person among you will eventually become a judge in the ways and methods of your own life, this provides a reason to even consider a sort of measurement in determining your own value.

We may better relate to the selling of your very own portion or shares of accumulated value you have experienced. You are devaluing your own worth in a judgmental, systematic tribunal of salvation. You may argue that you will not face condemnation because, '"I will always and forever be loved".'

This may lead to a construct in your mind of adopting these weaknesses as part of our composition and the confidence that eventually a rescue will come to place us back on track, in the right direction.

The greatest influence one can have is from a family unit. A nurturing father and mother, brothers and sisters present to interact with each other. The influence of a parent on a child is vital. The child must be brought up and raised properly, ready to face social interaction and society as a whole. One key element I learned when studying to be a project manager, is to develop strategies for successful completion and avoid having your project turn into chaos.

I'm not a parent but I'm sure that every parent practices obedience in their house.

I wonder how a parent manages a child that continues to disobey rules for developing and rearing for a successful outcome as a member of society.

A parent may consider a valuation system to determine how much to further continue with guidance and nurturing.

I'm sure a parent doesn't want to just give up, but if your guidance and teaching is not productive or is rejected, it most certainly will influence decisions to be made regarding the investment of time, resources and money.

By nature, we are inclined to sin and inherently seek a path which does not lead in the direction toward God. Since it is said that following such a path enables us so easily with levels of attraction and pleasure, it may even include deceit and false teaching. You begin to realize that it is not a path towards God and is considered to be in the wrong direction.

Eventually, you discover that your own worth is devalued or in terms to understand, it has affected your valuation for salvation. I believe it is known that we will all encounter moments of weakness which leads down a path in the wrong direction. This may be accounted for as an adjustment when it comes to measuring our value in our consideration to be saved from the consequences of travelling the wrong direction.

This is called risk. When analyzing the decisions made to move forward and choices you have made, or more fitting, the choices you have been given, you are evaluating the risk of any consequences that may result.

This gives "risk" a value and its worth. With all the careful rationale and calculation performed to make a decision, the outcome is unknown.

Not knowing the final solution to the equation, not knowing whether a higher power will honor the insurance claim and provide salvation. In order to hypothesize any predictive solutions, further study in risk analysis of salvation is required.

Being educated at a major University, I have a background in engineering, physics and astronomy and have studied the function of our physical world. It is rather complicated once you began to learn the elements of quantum mechanics and physics.

The main reason it becomes complex is because of true experiences known as a paradox. Simply defined by Webster, a paradox is a "a statement that is seemingly contradictory or opposed to common sense and yet is perhaps true".

I'm going to relate a very simple human function and explain how it can become rather complex when applying the science of different quantum states. Let's take vision, if your eyes function properly you are able to see where you are, directly in front you, but only if your eyes are open. You look down to the floor and see a coin, a deeper look shows it is a penny. This entire image is a reflection in the back of your retina. With your eyes open you can only see it with plenty of light for the reflection to take place. You have seen it and identified it is there on the floor. Basic theory of relativity explains that the penny is there and in your frame of reference. Questions arise when you study outside your frame of reference.

If someone else enters your frame, they should see the same thing, unless something different is being reflected on the back of the other person's retina or the lighting changes the image of the penny on the floor.

Then the question arises, "Is there a penny on the floor yes or no." The state of the penny in your frame is in a different state than the other person's frame of reference. This scenario creates a paradox and there is no way to accurately determine which state is true since they seem contradictory. This is science. It's way to explain existence with empirical formulation. But there was a time when science was considered heresy.

Christianity is a paradox. Religion has developed over the years from evangelicals like the apostle Paul.

When I arrived at the point of questioning the reason for the existence of a church, my thoughts were spurred when I began to see the number of churches everywhere around me. All different kinds of churches, little ones, big ones, all different kinds of denominations.

I thought, there are as many churches around as there are convenience and grocery stores. Further contemplation led to the cost of building a church because it would nice to build a house for myself and I started to figure out the cost of such a project. Just seeing the number of churches around being built and established, I started seeing these structures as a business, after all where was the money coming from to build and continue operating such a structure?

This is the point when I realized that everyone must have a growing concern to discern and validate that which exists in your environment and to confirm your material and spiritual convictions.

After studying how Christianity and the gospel spread throughout the world, I stepped back, and began to see how Christianity was being marketed to gain public favor, an emerging IPO (Initial Public Offering). There is a major issue that exists with this model. Christianity is not marketable, hence the paradox. I have experience in advertising, selling space and time.

I've produced it and I've sold it, and one thing I've learned is that the product itself is what makes it marketable, secondly the message and content on how it is delivered to the public.

The business is easier when there is a solid market and the seller has confidence in a reliable product.

To market Christianity, you have to create a selling point for salvation. In order to be saved, you have to relinquish everything and give up everything you own.

With my experience in business, this is a hard sell. Somehow this was accomplished because the religion is still around. It probably launched by offering other qualities in life that helped the needy or provided refuge.

This is where I begin to think how it developed spiritually over the years and I find that a collision occurs in the present, just by what I see represents it.

The selling point must have developed over the years from relinquishing all your possessions through the process of salvation (the Gospel) to something opposite, at the other end of the spectrum, happiness and joy perhaps. A celebration? What are we celebrating? Life or death.

Since I began writing, a lot of people have told me that life is about the choices we make. Pretty general statement, and I've heard it numerous times. After thinking deeply about this, I can't seem to accept it. We make choices all of the time. little ones, medium choices and really important choices.

To say that life is about the choices we make seems rather short-sided on the part of those trying to convey a message to you. It's as if they are saying the world is at your disposal, just pick and choose what you want. Does anyone believe that the world is at their disposal? I suppose it's that easy when this is actually true.

They are better off saying that life is about the choices given to you. If the choices included all of the different options available in the world, one could say "life is good." My current experience has not included that many choices. It's as if a fish bowl were handed to me and I was told to pick one.

Whether a business is trying to identify its next course of action, find the right personnel, or choose partners, there could be enormous pressure to do the right thing.

In business, choices are made every day involving very serious thought, rationality, and numbers. One of the most valuable assets in making wise and spirit-aligned decisions is spiritual instinct. That subtle feeling which is beyond the conscious mind, that which drives emotion and unconscious self-awareness. The revelation that trusting your own instincts provides more profound guidance.

Intuition is not just the idea that comes from our head or a hunch that comes from nowhere. It is communication with your soul and oneself, and manifests through signs from your body, feelings, and mind.

Giving attention to these signs may lead you in the right direction, a spiritual direction of what you really want and what you stand for in order to make more genuine and rewarding decisions in business. Placing a great amount of attention on intuition has its downside. Deep concentration aggravates stress and anxiety and our perception becomes narrow and fast, and there is a need to stop and clear your mind.

Finding time to relax can be as simple as taking several deep breaths, meditating or stepping away from the situation to focus on the moment. When you relax, you give your body permission to let go of associated stress and reduces an increase in cortisol which interferes with clear thinking.

Intuition is related to innovative thinking and heart-centered ideas which require rational thinking so that turmoil does not overshadow intuition. Try not to dismiss these feelings since they can further assist in sorting out difficult or unpleasant choices from more appetizing choices that align closer with your core identity.

## Inspirational Examples

It is important to realize that divine inspiration is an aspect of leadership linked to growth and the groups they lead, in addition to creating ideas with collaboration and empathy. A great number of stories can be told that elaborate divine inspiration in leadership.

One of the most striking stories perhaps is Jacinda Ardern, the former Prime Minister of New Zealand. The manner in which Ardern has navigated New Zealand through the coronavirus pandemic has been hailed as using the best empathetic communication strategy. Although, Ardern never said she received instructions from God, she did provide effective leadership during disasters and shared what others considered a "moral high ground" compared to typical political strategies.

The New Zealand PM Jacinda Ardern is chiefly credited for the success story of managing the pandemic and many felt her leadership appeared to be motivated by some kind of divine purpose by the way she actually cared for her people.

This proved to be a "moment of truth" by demonstrating the care and concern she showed as evidence of a leader who understands her staff. The ability of a leader to exemplify their core leadership skills can be defined as having a place to deliver a clear purpose.

Many leaders in history have even been more vocal to acknowledge that their success was divined by the Lord. The best example is Napoleon Bonaparte who believed he was anointed by fate to be a leader. Napoleon announced his mission and felt that God put him in the post to change the face of Europe. His meteoric ascent in revolutionary France, and later as Emperor, was characterized by audacity to which many believed that he was preordained. During his lifetime Napoleon defended his political ascendancy by stating that he was anointed by divine providence and that specific warfare triumphs were well orchestrated by God. He had absolute faith in his mission from God, he was confident and able to mobilize people to follow him.

In more modern leadership practices, the direct reference to divine intervention may not be so much present in literature, but stem from principles which go beyond mere strategies of management.

Some leaders inherently possess curiosity and empathy essential to learning about oneself like teamwork and having a profound respect toward others. Potential leaders acquire reflection and action as qualities considered to be divine intervention.

The individuals having these qualities are able to draw upon resources best described as being from "divine light" when confronted with ethical dilemmas in the current enterprise climate.

# Chapter 10: Building a Lasting Legacy with Faith

What constitutes a lasting legacy?

There are elements that make up a legacy that withstand over time and these elements are the basis of influence across generations. Part of this legacy is comprised of one's values combined with fundamental beliefs that shapes practice and decision-making throughout a lifetime. To build something that would endure, you need to know what you are for and what you are against and what would you like to be remembered for.

Just as important is the ability to achieve goals that are clearly stated and resonate with a set of values. It is not about what has been achieved, but how it has been achieved. These goals provide organization in accordance to the overall plan being implemented.

Helping people is another component of building a legacy that is worth mentioning. The impact or contribution that you make on the people around you is what causes ripples beyond the immediate community. When you give, show kindness or become a mentor by helping others, you indirectly create a lasting impression by using your own talent or assets. The wider reach of people you influence, the greater your impact will be.

Wealth allows you to carry out what God has called you to do, and part of that is passing along the knowledge to manage that wealth to future generations.

Making children and grandchildren appreciate the importance of money, money management, saving, and investing empowers them to replicate the successes made. The premise is to prepare and educate children for becoming "financially fit." This provides a guarantee that the next generation will be competent and resilient to steward wealth accumulated in the future.

**Biblical Principles & Theory**

One might have taken his inspiration from the words of **Proverbs 4:25–27**: *"Prevent your eyes from looking right and left; restrain your sight from observing what lies to the rear. Consider the ways for your feet and think it over and be firm in your steps. Therefore, do not go right or left; remove your foot from evil."*

Companies that are weak at the core of their organizational structure are at risk of breaking down at its foundation. It's as if they were built on shifting sand that can easily give in at any one time. I have come up with the saying, "We are only as good as our leaders."

Our destiny is played out in the future but is determined by actions taken in the present time. Jesus gives his followers this powerful principle to live by. In **Matthew 6:33** *"But seek ye first the kingdom of God and his righteousness, and all the rest will follow"*

Indeed, this verse carries important instructions. This scripture makes reference to God himself and His principles should come first. Believe His order and look to His kingdom first.

One practical application in business is doing the first thing that comes to mind. When a leader comprehends the order of things, the order of things become more comprehensible. A true leader should know well what he or she wants as well as to train others to know what they want.

When a company recognizes the talent available within the company and places each employee in a strategic position to fully utilize the gifts they have been given, productivity rises. The difficulties you confront are some of the things that will define your character. Doing all that is possible to overcome many adversities is the best way of showing people that any difficulties are not barriers but challenges. Mastery over challenges with determination provides examples of endurance, and together with an attitude of generosity, comprises an important aspect of a legacy that can withstand time. These actions whether in the form of time, money or information are common to the history of "giving" and creates a culture of helping others that will be remembered across generations.

A permanent impact is also one with regard to personal development and education that never ends.

In this regard, improving skills or processes through education and experience improves the impact of a legacy.

This unrelenting pursuit of personal development gives your efforts layers and substance and ensures that you are depositing into society something more valuable than money.

The relationships you build with people like family, friends and business associates have a tremendous bearing on how your legacy will be sustained. These are the relationships which give support, inspiration, and cooperation and increase the effectiveness of your endeavors.

Finally, creating an enterprise that has a purpose in life and endures the test of time is established by visioning, enduring and creating significant change to last a lifetime. Keep in mind the opportunities and pathways as always being accessible to the next generation, driven by knowledge and values that one shares, including finance literacy, courtesy, generosity as well as many others. By adopting these aspects, your legacy can be used to help and make the world a better place to live for generations to come.

**Final Thoughts**

It is more than just convincing oneself that it is possible to practice faith at work. In fact, it is a strategic tool which can transform a business if applied well.

When you decide to operate your business based on faith, you set up an operating system within which all your activities are directed and have a lasting beneficial effect on business, employees, consumers, and society as a whole.

One of the ways through which faith enriches business practices is being the provision of a foundation.

In **Proverbs 16:3**, we are encouraged by *"whatever you do, commit it to the Lord, and He will make your plans succeed."*

Praying before commencing a business venture may help a businessman because it helps to establish that the business venture is a divine endeavor. It can assist in providing direction to the enterprise. It provides the business owners with the ability to face challenges with some form of guarantee that the work effort is for the goodwill of society and create long-term stability and sustainability.

Faith also gives insight and directions in making decisions. As **James 1:5** teaches that if any of you lack wisdom, ask God who gives to all without reproof. This assurance enables corporate managers and owners to make ethical decisions in complex situations such as financial issues faced by employees and other stakeholders. When applying Christian theology to managing a company, it is not a wise thing to look for worldly wisdom, but the Word of God says, seek first the kingdom of God and all these things shall be added unto you. These are strong pillars that will provide proper wisdom to manage a company and not worldly advice.

Also, putting faith into business initiatives makes your business stronger. An entrepreneurial venture is not easy and one should not be surprised if he/she experiences some failures along the way.

In **Philippians 4:13** Paul said in his epistle to the Corinthians, *"I can do all things through Christ which strengthens me."*

Through faith, businesses and their owners can be strong to face all the odds, transform challenges into lessons, and endure difficult times encountered by any respective company.

Finally, integration of faith provides an achievement that goes beyond the issue of a profit-making venture.

**Colossians 3:23-24** urges us to *"do your very best, whatever you do, as for the Lord."*

When business owners are able to look at what they do as a service unto the Lord, they find a new meaning in what they do. This fulfillment creates passion and makes things work positively for the business and the lives it influences.

In conclusion, faith integrated into a business practice provides maximum, positive change by giving a company a foundation, knowledge, stability, a moral compass and meaning. It strengthens an individual to overcome hardships to provide services and improve their social doctrine as it exists. When faith is integrated with business, the end product is not just economic success, but a successful business entity that is Bible-honoring and socially relevant.

# About the Author

I'm Oscar Calderon, a firm believer that faith and business can work hand in hand. With a background in communications, astrophysics, and business, I've explored how integrity and morality can shape true success. In Spiritual Economy, I share insights from my spiritual journey, blending biblical wisdom with real-world strategies to help professionals lead and discern.

# Proof

www.ingramcontent.com/pod-product-compliance
Lightning Source LLC
Chambersburg PA
CBHW061652120626
46550CB00003B/915